TRASH TO TREASURE

EXPLORING A NEW WAVE OF ENTREPRENUERSHIP WITH WASTE

Dear Anna,
Thanks for all you
do to make the
world better!

KELSEY E. RUMBURG

Keep up the
great work!
Kelsey

NEW DEGREE PRESS

TRASH TO TREASURE

Exploring a New wave of Entreprenuership With Waste

ISBN		
	978-1-63676-594-5	*Paperback*
	978-1-63676-231-9	*Kindle Ebook*
	978-1-63676-233-3	*Ebook*

For Leila Janah, who taught me to see the value in everything.
Your spirit has guided this book. Let's change the world!

CONTENTS

We can end extreme poverty. And the best way is to give people economic agency through work. Work, for so many of us, means independence; it is the triumph of the human body and mind over all that is within our power to control.

—LEILA JANAH, *GIVE WORK*

INTRODUCTION

Imagine a grocery store full of weird-shaped produce: crooked carrots, brown-tinged broccoli, and little lemons. Feels strange, doesn't it?

But our produce doesn't grow perfectly shaped—in fact, according to the USDA, as much as 40 percent of food in the United States is wasted, with so-called ugly produce left in the field to rot or salvaged at pennies to the dollar for processed items, such as canned goods or frozen foods.[1]

Farming is hard and dirty work, and the margins are slim to begin with. So imagine having to leave half of what you produce in the field, or having it rejected by the market because it doesn't look like the perfect tomato, potato, or carrot. Even worse, imagine it's a good growing year and everyone has surplus supply, so you are unable to sell your produce to any market that's already inundated with supply.

---

1   "Food Waste FAQs," U.S. Department of Agriculture, accessed September 12, 2020.

Now what do you do with your produce? In some cases, you might be able to donate it. However, this has restrictions, such as minimum amounts and perishable item storage requirements, so donating isn't always possible. In most cases, it's left to rot in the field, left to fertilize the soil, and it's not utilized for all of the resources it took to actually grow it—the labor, energy, and water.

What if, instead, there was a way to get that produce to consumers willing to use it even though it's ugly or surplus? Several companies have popped up to combat this problem over the past few years. One of those companies, Hungry Harvest, has also taken great strides to combat issues accessing fresh produce in food deserts, aiming to solve two complex food-related issues at once.

Hungry Harvest's founder Evan Lunz highlights a key mindset shift that has occurred over the past decades. "I think our former generations would slap us across the face if they saw how much food is going to waste. Never before in history have we ever wasted this much food. Many parents and grandparents came to this country with little in their pocket and taught us the value of stretching the dollar. I'm not sure where that message got lost."

By embracing the idea that this wasted food was not waste at all, they ended up creating a rapidly growing company that is tackling issues of both food waste and food insecurity while still making a profit and paying workers fair wages. However, food waste isn't the only issue on our planet. Waste per person has rapidly increased in the past century, but few have gone so far as to see it as a resource from which to build a company. Evan could have built any company. He could have aspired to become the next Bill Gates or Jeff Bezos. Instead, he chose a different path—one that uses waste, in this case food waste, to build his company.

Trash is a human construct. In nature, there is no such thing as waste or trash, everything is cycled and reused. Trees in a forest may die, but they are not truly dead—they become home for insects, squirrels, and birds. As they decay, they fertilize the soil, providing vital nutrients for more trees to grow. Yet, human trash is a global phenomenon. And a very costly one at that. In America, approximately $200 billion dollars is spent annually for solid waste disposal.[2]

Edward Humes explains this best in *Garbology: Our Dirty Love Affair with Trash,* explaining:

> *Americans make more trash than anyone else on the planet, throwing away about 7.1 pounds per person per day, 365 days a year. Across a lifetime that rate means, on average, we are each on track to generate 102 tons of trash. Each of our bodies may occupy only one cemetery plot when we're done with this world, but a single person's 102-ton trash legacy will require the equivalent of 1,100 graves. Much of that refuse will outlast any grave marker, pharaoh's pyramid or modern skyscraper: One of the few relics of our civilization guaranteed to be*

---

2   Ann M. Simmons, "The world's trash crisis, and why many Americans are oblivious," *Los Angeles Times,* April 22, 2016.

recognizable twenty thousand years from now is the potato chip bag.[3]

Let's think about that for a second. One of the few relics of our civilization guaranteed to be recognizable twenty thousand years from now is the *potato chip bag.*

What? Is this how we want to be remembered?

Sadly, according to World Bank, by 2050, the world is expected to generate 3.40 billion tons of waste annually, increasing drastically from today's 2.01 billion tons.

While this may seem bleak, this is not a hopeless affair. There are ways to change, and even individuals making changes in their lives can make a difference. However, to truly be effective, larger collective change must occur. While some might argue that this might be for governments, nonprofits, or individuals to manage, the reality is that we all have a part to play. Additionally, businesses can, and should be, a part of the solution.

For the past two centuries, entrepreneurship and commerce has been focused on building. Henry Ford automated the manufacturing process to build more cars, Sam Walton built massive Walmart Stores, and Jeff Bezos has built the internet giant we know as Amazon. We admire these entrepreneurs for everything they have built. But we fail to see the

---

3   Edward Humes, *Garbology: Our Dirty Love Affair with Trash,* (New York: Avery, 2012), chap. 1, Kindle.

long-term impact of the trash they have created and to hold them accountable for the costs it takes to manage that waste.

Entrepreneurs are a resourceful bunch—they see the potential of underutilized resources. They see what currently is and transform it into something valuable for society, making a profit in doing so. In many ways, we have seen two amazing waves of entrepreneurs over the course of the industrial revolution.

First, there is the wave of automaters—epitomized by Henry Ford—who transformed labor as an underutilized resource with the assembly line. Next, we have the wave of tech entrepreneurs, who saw the potential of technology and the internet far before others anticipated its power—building massive companies as a result. The tech era of entrepreneurship includes the likes of Bill Gates, Steve Jobs, and Mark Zuckerberg.

Now there is a third wave rising. They are not builders. They are not destroyers. They are not automaters.

They are thrifters, recyclers, and creators. They do not build exclusive clubs, they invite all. They choose the hard path instead of the fast path.

These are the regenerators. Regenerators don't just solve problems or outsmart their competitors. They have the courage to see a better version of the world and are willing to wade through the murky waters to see that come to be true. They follow a unique framework that we often fail to see today—they:

1. Recognize the intrinsic value of trash—a jar isn't just a jar—it has value in that it can store a variety of items.
2. Apply this thinking to other areas where they see trash—a plastic wrapper is meant to keep food safe, but what other value could it have?
3. Start to wonder how many resources it took to create their "trash." How many resources did it take to produce that jar or wrapper?
4. Develop a new appreciation for the value of their trash.
5. Begin to brainstorm and create new ways to reuse the item.
6. Look for ways to use this more broadly in their life.
7. Understand this is a journey. They don't keep everything, but they try to find creative and community-based ways to solve their problems instead of selecting the most convenient option. This leads them to finding business-based approaches to solve these issues.

These steps have been a part of my journey. A few years ago, as I went for a quiet walk down the beach in the Philippines, I was struck by how much plastic I saw floating in the water and along the shoreline. Indeed, less than a month later Boracay—the popular tourist island I had visited—was closed for several months to clean up all of the garbage and damage done to the once pristine island.

I had always been raised to be resourceful and value the gifts of our planet, but it wasn't until that moment that it truly struck me how much damage we were doing in our individual choices as humans. On my flight home, I started to grapple with the idea of trash and our disposable culture.

Was there ever going to be a way to combat the damage we have done and to prevent additional damage from occurring?

As an individual, I have sought to replace single use plastic items, reuse everything I can, and reduce my trash footprint. However, individual actions can only go so far. Much like an individual stone falling into water, ripples can spread far and wide. I started to look for ways to scale this into my life and became aware of the brave heroes fighting this challenge. Realizing I could use my talents to amplify their incredible work, this book began to take shape.

My research led me to a new realization. Third-wave entrepreneurs don't build. They rebuild. They see "trash" as a resource—valuable for its inherent properties—and find creative and resourceful ways to use it to build businesses. As I have met more and more of these founders, I realized they were not different or special in terms of the resources they've had in life, they have simply used them differently.

Indeed, I realized we can all be regenerators. Whether you are an entrepreneur, a businessperson, a student, a parent, a teacher, an innovator, or a concerned caretaker of our planet thinking about how to have a positive impact on the world around us, this book is for you. We can all take responsibility for the sustainability of our planet. As entrepreneurs and aspiring entrepreneurs, we can build a new economy with companies embracing a regeneration mindset. But this is not the only thing we need.

As innovators, policy makers, academics, and researchers, we must remove barriers to utilizing trash as a core component in these forward-thinking businesses and we must actively encourage ideas and businesses tackling the global challenge of waste to emerge. As humans—parents, children, siblings, teachers, students, and friends—we must encourage creativity and resourcefulness in problem-solving, challenging the accepted norms and most convenient solutions with those that resourcefully use what we have.

As an in-depth exploration of the founders and entrepreneurs who are driving this new wave of business, this book explores the intersections of the environmental and economic challenges of trash while providing real world examples for tackling this global problem. By the time you finish reading this, you'll be seeing trash as a valuable resource and looking for new ways to use it in life and business!

PART I

THE REGENERATIVE MINDSET

Garbage has become one of the most accurate measures of prosperity in twenty-first-century America and the world.

—EDWARD HUMES, *GARBOLOGY: OUR DIRTY LOVE AFFAIR WITH TRASH*

CHAPTER 1

DISPOSABLE MINDSET 101

WHERE IS AWAY?

Let's take a little field trip! We're going to sail back to 2019 and hop aboard the *Resolute* to hit the high seas with SoulBuffalo—an experiential learning company for top executives. A writer for *Outside* magazine tagged along to describe this field trip, which included several executives from companies that use substantial amounts of plastic and environmental leaders—all sailing in close quarters.

The *Resolute* does not head toward some relaxing private island. No, it's off to the North Atlantic Gyre—one of the unique places in the ocean where several currents meet and circulate. Upon arrival at the Gyre, the adventurous executives geared up to go snorkeling—not to see a rare species of seahorse, but to see an abundance of plastic. Notably, if you shake a piece of sargassum—a type of seaweed—you can create a real-life snow globe. Imagine being surrounded by tiny pieces of microplastics as your swim through the water.

The purpose of this field trip was not to relax and have fun. The purpose was to bring executives from large companies—like The Dow Chemical Company, Nestlé Waters, and Coca-Cola—face to face with a problem their companies have helped to create—plastic pollution. The North Atlantic Gyre, as well as the other ocean gyres, have become an alphabet soup of plastic—bottle caps, fishing nets, jugs, and micro-plastic pieces from plastic bags and other single-use containers—all swirling around bountifully in the ocean.

"Seeing all that plastic speaks for itself. How do we close the loop? We can design lighter bottles. We can do it in ways that make recycling more efficient," said David Tulauskas, who is the Chief Sustainability Officer at Nestlé Waters North America—which produces 1.7 million metrics tons of plastic packaging each year for its portfolio of bottled-water brands. David continues by saying, "We own that. But we need to move faster and farther with the use of recycled content, and there's great partners here for that."[4]

All of these plastics have ended up in the North Atlantic Gyre because they were thrown away. But as we are beginning to see, there is should read *away away* our planet.

---

4   Rowan Jacobsen, "An Ocean Plastics Field Trip for Corporate Executives," *Outside,* August 8, 2019.

We need things we don't really need, and then we need to throw away things we no longer need. How does that make sense?

LIVING A SIMPLE LIFE:

There's an old adage "money doesn't buy happiness," but is a simpler life a happier one? A 1978 study published in the *Journal of Personality and Social Psychology* compared the happiness of several people—those who won the lottery and others who had a life-altering accident that resulted in them requiring a wheelchair for the remainder of their life. Right after these life-changing moments, the lottery winners were generally happier. But, interestingly, a year after winning the lottery or the accident, those who learned to use a wheelchair actually report higher levels of happiness than those who won the lottery.[5]

This is making a fundamental assumption that basic needs of food, water, shelter, and safety were met before and after these occurrences, but we can see where money is not necessarily the source of happiness.

Combining this research, we see that happiness comes from how we live—not what we have. We now face a tipping point where we must face our true values. When we purchase items, are we doing so because we need them, or are we doing so

---

5   P. Brickman, D. Coates, and R. Janoff-Bulman, "Lottery winners and accident victims: is happiness relative?" *Journal of Personality and Social Psychology* 36, no. 8, (1978): 917–927.

thoughtlessly because of some underlying fear or anger that we are coping with through retail therapy?

TRASH TALK:
The past decades have allowed us to live in relative abundance in comparison to the scarcity of the Great Depression and World Wars. We rebuilt the economy of the 1950s based on hefty consumption, embracing an idea of the good life we often still strive for today.[6]

Many assume economists study how to grow the economy and make more money. In reality, economists study how to use scarce resources to support humanity. In our world, cheap resources come at a high cost. Some goods we buy daily as consumers are actually artificially cheap, either because of subsidies or because their production does not take into account externalities—such as environmental damage from pollution or social damage caused by living in poverty. For instance, to make a pair of socks that only costs the end buyer three dollars, the true costs must come from elsewhere— either by paying workers low wages, transporting it using cheap fuel, or buying cheap raw materials. In most cases, it's a combination of these. Yes, the consumer wins by getting a three-dollar pair of socks. However, if the trade-off is that they have asthma from exposure to pollution as a result of the transportation of the socks, is it truly a win?

Okay, enough talk about economics. Let's talk trash!

---

6   "The Rise of American Consumerism," PBS: Public Broadcasting Service, accessed September 12, 2020.

A few years ago, I started to wonder about trash. I joined beach cleanups and worked to reduce the plastic I saw continuously washing up on the shore, but I questioned whether it would actually make a difference. I did my best to recycle properly and reduce my consumption, but still the question of what could truly be done to reduce the planet's trash gnawed at me.

As I dug down deeper, I asked myself, "What is trash really?" and even more importantly, "Why on earth do we buy and consume so much stuff?" With new curiosity, I researched what we call trash to understand why it exists and permeates our culture.

This wasn't the first time I questioned our society's relationship with waste—I realized I'd seen an example of this in my own life before.

Just after graduating college, I set off for a few months to travel the world. I know I am extremely privileged to have that opportunity, and I used money I had earned working through high school and college. I took with me nothing but a carry-on sized backpack. Yes, a carry-on. I didn't want to have to worry about losing my bag in the middle of my trip, so I packed light. During this trip, I learned a lot about how our way of living impacts our society.

I always assumed I needed many things: shampoo, a curling iron, a variety of clothing, and a bunch of other stuff. I assumed that *stuff* made me who I am. This trip made me realize very quickly that I am just as happy, if not happier, with far less items and far more experiences. I quickly real-ized there are very few necessities I have in terms of items.

I wondered why we must have so many items. If I dream to have a big house and fill it with stuff, will I really find happiness?

I explored this more and discovered some very interesting things. First, our love of living large is reflected in our society in house sizes. Believe it or not, according to AEI, "Over the last 42 years, the average new US house has increased in size by more than 1,000 square feet, from an average size of 1,660 square feet in 1973 to 2,687 square feet last year. Amazingly, the average amount of living space per person in a new house has nearly doubled in just the last 42 years!"[7]

The question then becomes "how are we filling all of this space?" I have a few theories—the rise of the "discounting" culture and the rise of the advertising industry. Discount stores offer consumers the high of a dopamine hit when they get a good deal—even if they didn't need that item in the first place. Still, they got a prize in the form of knowing they got a reward, and they got it cheap.[8]

Additionally, the plethora of incessant advertising around us is designed to make us feel cognitive dissonance. Meaning

7   Mark J. Perry, "New US homes today are 1,000 square feet larger than in 1973 and living space per person has nearly doubled," American Enter-prise Institute (blog), June 5, 2016, accessed September 12, 2020.

8   "How a great sale affects your brain," CBS News, December 15, 2013, accessed September 12, 2020.

we are missing something in our life—even when we are perfectly happy—to get us to spend money. Just yesterday, I was listening to music online and an ad came up from Starbucks for a caramel Frappuccino explaining how sweet and delicious it would be. All of a sudden, here I was thinking about how much I wanted a Starbucks caramel-swirl Frappuccino. The kicker? I don't even like caramel-swirl Frappuccinos! But man, did it sound good the way they advertised it.

We work hard for our money, but what are we really working for in the end? Money gives us the ability to buy things, but what we buy actually has the ability to impact our happiness. A study published in 2020 in the *Journal of Experiential Social Psychology* finds that spending on experiential purchases—such as travel and entertainment—result in a much higher level of satisfaction than material purchases—such as fashion or gadgets.[9] Why does consumption persist? According to a 2015 research study at the University of Victoria, Canada, "What has been referred to as 'affluenza' (Hamilton & Denniss, 2005) is an addictive condition whereby many are substituting their true needs with addictive consumeristic behaviors."[10]

Our relationship with trash parallels our relationship with consumption—the more we consume, the more trash we

9   Amit Kumar, Matthew A. Killingsworth, and Thomas Gilovich, "Spending on doing promotes more moment-to-moment happiness than spending on having," *Journal of Experimental Social Psychology*, 99, May 2020.

10 Duncan M. Taylor and David Segal, "Healing Ourselves and Healing the World: Consumerism and the Culture of Addiction," *Journal of Future Studies* 19 (2015): 77–86.

inevitably produce. By becoming truly conscious of our needs and wants, we can cut through the advertising and the excessive consumption to find a better relationship with our material processions, trash, and likely even our relationships.

WHAT EVEN IS TRASH?

Often, when we think of a leader fighting against the idea of trash, we picture a hippie with long hair who would fit in more at Woodstock than in a boardroom. What we don't realize is that companies repurposing waste run across a large spectrum, as do their leaders. Dr. Andrew Dent has dedicated his life to helping companies solve their materials problems, many of which involve elements of sustainability. After receiving his PhD in Materials Science at University of Cambridge, he joined Material ConneXion, where he now serves as Executive Vice President of Research.

In his career, he has seen a transition from materials science—focused on cost and durability—to adding an additional element of sustainability. Indeed, when one of his clients, Puma, asked him to come up with an alternative to their shoe box, he and his team came up with an even more radical solution: a bag, which could be repurposed easily and required less resources to produce than cardboard.

But for him, the real enemy is trash.

> I wish we stopped calling it trash. I mean, it's just it's the wrong word. It suggests that it has no value. And I think that is wrong. It's just the way that it is, you know. I think in one of my talks, I said that nature produces zero

trash, because everything it produces, every bit of waste, is used by something else. So I think we need to sort of approach it in that way. As I think about the number of things I put into my waste, I think, 'You know what, that will probably be used in some way.'

As we start to become more aware of what we see as trash, we begin to realize that much of it—from plastic to textiles to food scraps—can be given a second life. It may be easy to tell ourselves that we live in a world of abundant resources and don't need to worry about the one plastic thing we throw away. Still, reflecting on our relationship with waste is a key part of the journey in becoming both a regenerative entrepreneur, and, more importantly, a mindful consumer.

HOW DID WE GET HERE?

"The objects flying through the air in this picture would take 40 hours to clean—except no housewife need bother," reads a 1955 article in *Life* magazine titled "Throwaway Living."[11] Featured in this article is a photo of a family surrounded by throwaway conveniences: plastic plates to diapers to dog bowls. The article praises the convenience of single-use items that save housewives time by not having to clean them. Plastic became cheaper, lives became busier, dual-income households became more prominent, and something had to change. Time is money, and with time rapidly becoming a precious commodity, convenience and ease eclipsed quality, durability, and resourcefulness to epitomize success.

---

11   "Throwaway Living," *Life*, August 1955, 43.

According to the EPA, the amount of waste each American produces per day has nearly doubled since 1960. "The generation rate in 1960 was just 2.68 pounds per person per day. It increased to 3.66 pounds per person per day in 1980. In 2000, it reached 4.74 pounds per person per day and then decreased to 4.69 pounds per person per day in 2005. The generation rate was 4.51 pounds per person per day in 2017, which was one of the lowest generation rates since 1990."[12]

As our population continues to grow and each person produces more waste, what are we going to do with it all? Many populous states already sell their trash to other less populous states, but our trash volumes are increasing at an alarming rate that no state can handle.[13]

Our throwaway culture comes at a cost and has been highly criticized for its environmental and social consequences. These criticisms come from a variety of leaders, including economists, activists, and even religious leaders.

The *Economist* reports several key points on this topic:

- Why does America produce so much more rubbish? The difference is that in Europe and Japan it is manufacturers, rather than consumers, who are held responsible (via taxes on packaging waste) for the cost of processing the

12 "National Overview: Facts and Figures on Materials, Wastes and Recycling," United States Environmental Protection Agency, accessed September 13, 2020.

13 Lisa Iannucci, "Where Does the Garbage Go?" The Cooperator New York, September 2006, accessed September 13, 2020.

packaging used to wrap their goods. This gives them an incentive to use less of it.

- One of the biggest drains on profitability on any company is the materials, resources, and time wasted due to inefficiencies. The clearest physical manifestation of inefficiency is the amount of materials that companies send to either landfills or incinerators. All those resources entered the company's production chain with value, but leave it with none.
- "Waste is a resource in the wrong place" is a refrain that is gaining traction.
- By reducing the creation of waste and keeping it in its originally anticipated place as an input, rethinking waste as a resource to sell or extract value from, or adopting more circular processes, American companies have significant opportunities to put waste in its right place.[14]

In addition to this, several environmental activists have criticized our culture for promoting consumption and waste creation. Elizabeth Zimmerman, a certified environmental professional, points out:

> *"Planned obsolescence" is not a myth. It is a manufacturing philosophy developed in the 1920's and 1930's, when mass production became popular. The goal is to make a product or part that will fail, or become less desirable over time or after a certain amount of use. This pressures the consumer to buy again. Planned obsolescence does keep costs down. Instead of making an expensive product that will last a long time, businesses produce*

---

14   "Talking trash," *The Economist* Technology Quarterly, June 2, 2012.

more affordable, disposable items. In addition, tech-
nological advances are occurring at a breakneck pace.
Some electronic items have become so inexpensive that
it is cheaper to replace them than to repair them. Labor
and parts are pricey. Few consumers would pay $50 or
more to repair a broken VCR, when they can purchase
a brand new DVD player for the same amount.[15]

In producing items to have a limited life, we inherently produce more trash. National Geographic is also highly critical
of this, pointing out our limited resources and the effects of
our disposable mindset:

As a planet, we have finite materials–oil, metals, miner-
als and so on–available to us just once. Using them more
sparingly and slowly merely delays the date at which we
will exhaust them. We cannot continue in this linear
fashion. Using less is not a solution, it just buys you time.
The world's current take-make-dispose linear economy is
outdated. It is also the root cause of some of today's most
challenging problems. Earth faces a waste plastic crisis
that no amount of well-intentioned clean-ups can solve.[16]

Clearly, the environmental costs of waste are steep, but the
costs don't stop there. Pope Francis has widely shared his
criticism of our throw-away culture. "An economic system
detached from ethical concerns," he warned, "does not bring

---

15   Elizabeth A. Zimmerman, "How We Became a Throw-away Society," *Our*
      Better Nature (blog), April 4, 2008.

16   Ellen MacArthur, "Why our throwaway culture has to end," *National*
      Geographic, June 6, 2018.

about a more just social order, but leads instead to a 'throw-away' culture of consumption and waste. In the end, it is not simply a matter of 'having more,' but 'being more'," the Pope said, underscoring the need for renewing hearts and minds so that the human person may always be placed at the centre of social, cultural and economic life.[17] Many other religions and life philosophies also underscore the importance of not succumbing to greed and attachment to material goods.

OUR DISPOSABLE MINDSET COSTS US MORE THAN MONEY

While it may seem convenient and normal, our disposable mindset comes at a high cost to our environment, economy, and society.

Environmentally, according to a study done by the University of Georgia, eighteen billion pounds of plastic trash winds up in our oceans each year. To put that in perspective, it's enough trash to cover every *foot* of coastline around the world with five full trash bags of plastic…compounding *every* year.[18]

Let's go back to the field trip we went on at the beginning of this chapter to the North Atlantic Gyre, now a snow globe of microplastics. The outlook of our plastic consumption is very bleak. According to an article by CNN:

---

17   Robin Gomes, "Pope: economics without ethics leads to 'throw-away' culture," *Vatican News*, November 11, 2019.

18   Dianna Parker, "Why is plastic marine debris so common?", produced by Kurt Mann for Ocean Today, video, 2:22, accessed September 14, 2020.

Nearly every piece of plastic ever made still exists today. More than five trillion pieces of plastic are already in the oceans, and by 2050 there will be more plastic in the sea than fish, by weight, according to the Ellen MacArthur Foundation. [Additionally,] some 8 million tons of plastic trash leak into the ocean annually, and it's getting worse every year. Americans are said to use 2.5 million plastic bottles every hour.[19]

Perhaps most interestingly, though, is not just that our disposable mindset costs us our natural environment and our wallets, but it actually costs us our individual human connection. In a research study conducted at University of Kansas & University of Dayton, researchers discovered a correlation between a disposable mindset toward objects and that extending to personal relationships:

The perception of objects as disposable is associated with perceiving friends the same way. A personal history of greater mobility is tied to a higher readiness to dispose of objects and also close social ties like friendships and romantic relationships. Increasing the sense of residential mobility also boosts a person's willingness to dispose of both objects and personal relationships.[20]

---

19 Nick Paton Walsh, Ingrid Formanek, Jackson Loo and Mark Phillips, "Plastic Island: How our throwaway culture is turning paradise into a graveyard," CNN, accessed September 14, 2020.

20 University of Kansas, "Throwaway culture can include friendships, researcher says," ScienceDaily, accessed September 14, 2020.

Let's step back and look at the big picture. Our oceans are being choked by plastic, from reefs that feel more like New Year's Eve in Time Square with plastic confetti floating around than lively and abundant natural wonders of the world, to sea turtles and whales washing ashore, unable to properly digest food because their stomachs are full of plastic. It's a grim reality for our ocean life, but sadly this doesn't stop at the shoreline. Fish consume tiny plastic particles called microplastics and are then caught for both human and animal consumption. But before you say, "That's fine, I don't like sushi anyway, so it doesn't affect me," try to think about the fact that microplastics don't just occur in our oceans, but also in our freshwater lakes and streams. Do you really want to drink water with microplastic pieces in it? I sure as h*ll don't.

If this sounds alarming, good, it should! We are drowning in our own waste as a planet right now, and if we don't make some big changes, the future is grim.

Our perception of waste affects our planet, our pocket, and our very ability to build healthy relationships with each other—which in turn perpetuates our need to buy things to fill this void. When we find ways to combat this—not only for the sake of our society, but for our very selves—we can grow and build a better world.

THERE IS HOPE!
Despite all of this information regarding the detriments of our disposable culture, there are movements working to change it, such as:

- utilitarian living
- zero-waste living
- tiny house living

While these are a great inspiration for changing our culture, not everyone can implement such a major shift in lifestyle. Furthermore, while these movements address individual consumption, they do not address large scale consumption by businesses and organizations. As reported in the *Economist*, the burden of waste reduction cannot rest solely on the consumer or recycling collections, which require substantial scale to be viable.

Consumers are, of course, a part of the solution. But we, as a society—businesses, governments, NGOs, and consumers—are all responsible for making the change. In this book, we'll focus on the businesses that incorporate waste in their production. However, there are certainly many more examples of multi-stakeholder engagement for waste reduction, particularly in Northern Europe.

LESSONS FROM THE DISPOSABLE MINDSET

We have one planet. What can we learn from our disposable mindset so that we can find a new path forward? For me, there are a few key lessons that are vital here:

1. What we need and what we want are different things.
2. Our economy is based on rapid consumption—we can change this with our actions and our consumption habits.
3. A disposable mindset isn't just an environmental problem—it's an economic and societal problem as well.

4. Living with less is a great first step, but we need large scale change. Entrepreneurs are often at the forefront of large-scale change, and we are seeing entrepreneurs and companies emerge who thwart the idea of the disposable mindset. We have the ability to emulate their actions and amplify this movement.

This book will tackle the last point, but we cannot move forward with building regenerative businesses until we have accepted the other points from an individual and societal standpoint to move away from a disposable mindset.

CHAPTER 2

SMART PEOPLE SHOULD BUILD THINGS— FROM TRASH

Building a house from the ground up is hard. Decorating an elaborate wedding cake is hard. Starting a company is hard.

Why are these things hard? They don't follow a linear path, and they aren't something most people normally do each day. Builders spend years learning to build houses and hone their craft to make it look easy. Bakers become masters at making wedding cakes. Entrepreneurs learn to embrace the uncertainty of the survival of their companies and push forward to solve the problems they see in the world.

Entrepreneur and former presidential candidate, Andrew Yang, knows what it takes to tackle large problems with creative solutions. When he founded Venture for America—a nonprofit that aims to support entrepreneurship in emerging start-up ecosystems—not only did he not follow a linear path, he blazed one of his own. Trailblazing is, in fact, hard. In his book *Smart People Should Build Things*, Yang offers advice for recent college graduates, "One of the most frequently pursued paths for achievement-minded college seniors is to spend several years advancing professionally and getting trained and paid by an investment bank, consulting firms, or law firms. Then, the thought process goes, they can set out to do something else with some exposure and experience under their belts." Yang writes, "People are generally not making lifelong commitments to the field in their own minds. They're 'getting some skills' and making some connections before figuring out what they really want to do."[21]

The problem with this mindset, however, is that when we finally figure out what we want to do, we have grown accustomed to the lifestyle we have. There are financial and social risks in trying something new and failing, and we are not always willing to take these risks to pursue our passion. We might have a family we need to support with a stable income, or need a company-provided health insurance, or fear the shame of failure. Whatever the reason, the stakes often become higher.

The rate of entrepreneurship has declined substantially over the past decades in the US. This decline damages our economy. A 2014 study from the University of Maryland on the role of entrepreneurship in job creation found, "Startups and

---

21   Andrew Yang, *Smart People Should Build Things* (New York: HarperCollins, 2014), Kindle.

high-growth firms account for about seventy percent of firm-level gross job creation in a typical year."[22]

For job creation to continue, we need passionate leaders willing to take risks and start companies, or expand into new areas and businesses within their existing firms. Without new companies and ideas, we cannot innovate and change.

CHANGE IS NECESSARY—RIDING THE WAVES IS A CHOICE

I often sit and reflect near the beach—the waves subtly rolling up to the shore, sometimes barely noticeable, and sometimes in large white caps that remind one how fierce the ocean can be. As I sit and watch, I realize this is much like life—every wave different and changing, sometimes calm, sometimes harsh. I understand, now, why surfing and kite surfing are popular—they force you to become one with the waves, to adapt and move with them, rather than trying to control and change them. Entrepreneurship, particularly regenerative entrepreneurship, requires us to learn to surf.

The waves are sort of predictable, but you don't exactly know how things are going to go until you are in the middle of them. It's scary, exhilarating, and challenging, but that's what makes it so much fun!

---

22   Ryan Decker, John Haltiwanger, Ron Jarmin, and Javier Miranda, "The Role of Entrepreneurship in US Job Creation and Economic Dynamism," *Journal of Economic Perspectives* 28, no. 3 (2014): 3–24.

As I apply this more broadly in my life, I let go of the outcome I hope or expect, and instead enjoy the waves as they come—large or small. As I speak with founders, particularly regenerative founders, I see they have this certain way of accepting the waves—knowing they cannot change them, but they simply want to surf them. Learning to accept change is a powerful tool—one that helps to continuously adjust as challenges arise, and see potential everywhere, even when others only see waste.

LOOK FOR THE POTENTIAL IN EVERYTHING

How do we actually become better at riding the waves and adapting to change? Here are a few strategies that are very powerful.

- I often hear about problem-solving as a highly sought-after skillset these days. What does problem-solving actually mean? In the context of most jobs, it typically means coming up with a solution quickly. However, problem-solving is more complex. It entails learning how to ideate and find what solved actually looks like—not just a short-term solution. IDEO has several great resources on this.
- Reflect on the life you actually want to have. A house, no matter how big or beautiful it is, is still empty without others to fill it. Find happiness and meaning in yourself rather than in external situations.
- Realize every small action adds up—not everyone has to start a regenerative company, but choosing who we buy from, how we consume, and how we influence others to do the same is just as important.

ISN'T BUILDING SOMETHING DIFFICULT?

Probably. But nothing worth doing is easy, right?

I never expected to be writing a book about trash. I was lucky enough to take some sustainability courses during college and have some great professors who encouraged me to look for ways to use it in my career. But when I went into a large corporation, I realized just how difficult that was going to be. I tried to stay current on sustainability related topics that interested me—such as impact investing, conscious consumption, and the circular economy. Still, I felt myself losing focus and getting easily distracted by other things—like travel, partying, and other daily dramas. I realized I would need to open myself up to finding the life I actually wanted, and that might mean a very different path.

After some tears, thinking, meditation, prayer, and conversations, I decided to leave my nice life of adventure. I took a substantial pay cut and joined Venture for America (VFA) to go work in start-ups. I will never forget how in the course of one weekend, I woke up in my own beautiful apartment in Singapore where I had been working, flew home to the USA, and ended up back in a shared college dorm a day later for VFA's Training Camp—an intensive five-week summer program to prepare for life in start-ups. I can't tell you how many times I asked that weekend if I was crazy for making the choice I did. Many people dream of the life I had—working as an expat, getting to travel the world, being comfortable. I loved it too, but I somehow knew it wasn't my final path. So, there I was, sleeping in a dorm in Detroit and trying to figure out what on earth I had gotten myself into. Fortunately, my roommate turned out to be great and it did work out, but not in any way shape or form like I had imagined when I set out. And that's kind of the whole point.

Venture for America, founded by Andrew Yang, is a two-year fellowship program to create an inclusive entrepreneurship community and help recent college graduates move along a path to entrepreneurship by connecting them with jobs in one of fourteen cities with emerging start-up ecosystems in the US. These cities suffer from brain-drain, meaning their talented and educated youth move to San Francisco or New York after college to join start-ups, leaving a void of talent to support the community. With that said, there are great underutilized resources in these cities, and great entrepreneurs know how to find ways to use them.

Joining this fellowship has exposed me to many wonderful people and opportunities, but it has also allowed me the space to find my own path—rather than trying to follow the ladder to move my way up. It has forced me to face a lot of challenges and my biggest fears: failing, losing a job, and moving home to live with my parents (who are great roommates!). It has also taught me that hard things are worth it if you believe in them—and I deeply believe in building things from trash and creating a more circular economy.

So here I am, writing a book about it. Ask any writer and they will tell you that writing is difficult, and it sucks; but not writing is far, far worse. This idea chose me to bring it to life, and I must honor it.

Just as the waves flow to the shore—creating and then receding to form a new wave—so too can our economy. I personally don't think about the circular economy as a circle, but rather like waves in the ocean. For waves, the water takes a different shape, curving into a crest as it nears the shore, crashing on to the sand, and then drawing back into the depths. But, in all of this, the water doesn't lose its value, or truly change its shape. A circular economy can still have strong waves in the form of items and value creation, but it also draws the resources it uses back into it, continually re-circulating them into more waves. The energy produced regenerates new waves, building rather than destroying the planet for future generations.

Like building a house and making an elaborate wedding cake, building this type of economy is certainly very hard—but worth it.

RIDING THE WAVES
Can you actually make money from trash? Is that even possible? At a large scale?

Yes! Let's take TerraCycle for example.

TerraCycle isn't your average company. Walk around the office headquarters, and you find an array of mismatched secondhand desks, walls of upcycled records and water bottles, and a multitude of other *trash* re-purposed into office furniture and decoration. Sound like some Portland hipster's dream UX/UI design firm? Maybe, but you would be shocked to know this is not some little group of hippies living in a commune—it's big business.

Located in sunny Trenton, New Jersey, TerraCycle was founded in 2001 with one key mission: eliminate the idea of waste. The founder, Tom Szaky, a college student at the time, collected plastic bottles of all sorts, cleaned and refilled them with fertilizer made from worm refuse, and then relabeled and sold them for consumption—saving on the costly process of breaking down a plastic bottle to be reformed into another shape, and eliminating substantial amounts of waste.

Buoyed by this early success—but recognizing that there were limits in just selling worm fertilizer—TerraCycle continued to push the limits on the idea of what could be recycled, and what creative solutions it could find to eliminate waste by reusing, upcycling, and recycling products deemed unrecyclable. They started collecting packaging for companies including Clif & Honest tea and evolved from there. Today, they recycle anything that is shipped to them. Yes, they find a way to repurpose, upcycle, or recycle *everything*.

Over the years, TerraCycle's business model has morphed a few times, but they have built a large, profitable business based on the idea of eliminating waste. They've taken investment to scale more rapidly. According to Crunchbase, they closed a Series A in 2006 and additional funding in 2010.[23] They are still privately held, but Recycling Today points out that in 2018 they did qualify with the SEC for a twenty-five-million-dollar Regulation A capital raise.[24] The additional capital allowed them to add both additional products

---

23   "TerraCycle," Crunchbase, accessed September 15, 2020.

24   Megan Workman (ed.), "SEC qualifies $25 million Regulation A capital raise for TerraCycle US," *Recycling Today*, January 18, 2018.

and services, and also possibly acquire others in the space. Indeed, in 2018, TerraCycle had over twenty million dollars in revenue and $1.1 million in net profit, demonstrating that you really can make green from green.[25]

What helped make TerraCycle become successful?

1. In an interview with Business Insider, Tom explained that they haven't spent a dime on marketing. Seriously, nothing. Word of mouth, PR, and advocacy have been their biggest growth tools. Do something cool and innovative and people tend to listen.[26]
2. They have pivoted their model a few times. As a start-up, TerraCycle had to pivot a few times in terms of finding a scalable model to support its mission, but in doing so was able to achieve greater success.
3. Growth took time. In today's fast-paced, rapidly changing world, it's easy to want growth and success to be viral and exponential. But in this case, it's taken nearly two decades for TerraCycle to grow to this scale in a more measured and sustainable pace.
4. IT IS POSSIBLE! Yes, it truly is possible to build a trash-based business.

Currently, TerraCycle works with a variety of brands to collect their packaging and remake it into their products. For instance—as explained in a blog post—they worked with Head & Shoulders® to create a bottle for their products that

---

25   "TerraCycle," Start Engine, accessed October 10, 2020.

26   Kim Bhasin, "The Incredible Story of How TerraCycle CEO Tom Szaky Became a Garbage Mogul," *Business Insider*, August 29, 2011.

was made from recycled beach plastic.[27] Consumers, particularly millennials seeking ways to reduce their footprint, are often willing to pay marginally more for products that help the planet, so this type of model works well for both TerraCycle and large, name brand clients.

Continued success rests on a few assumptions. First, as mentioned in the Business Insider interview, there is the assumption that consumers will continue to value brands and products that do the right thing—like using recycled bottles.[28] While this has become a substantial trend—with upward of one in three millennials purchasing products for their mission—consumer preferences can always shift. For name brands, this is as much a marketing ploy (some might say greenwashing) as it is about reducing their footprint, but it does bring awareness to the substantial issue of waste on the planet. However, it remains to be seen if consumer preferences for these types of products will continue to support this. Second, it rests on the idea that consumption habits, particularly for name brands, will stay the same. Grocery Dive explains that many competitors are popping up to rival both name brands and reinvent how consumers shop—even for groceries and household goods. While some consumers are loyal to brands, many may start to value the private labeled products that companies like Public Goods or Thrive

---

27 "Ocean Pollution Doesn't Wash Away'," TerraCycle Blog (blog), November 26, 2019, accessed September 15, 2020.

28 Kim Bhasin, "The Incredible Story of How TerraCycle CEO Tom Szaky Became a Garbage Mogul," *Business Insider*, August 29, 2011.

produce, thus eliminating a revenue stream for TerraCycle if not managed properly.[29]

There is one outstanding question: is TerraCycle really the most sustainable option? In short—sometimes. Eliminating waste by recycling is a very important issue, but it does perpetuate one problem—consumption. By providing an outlet for things like wrappers and plastic bags to be recycled, it allows using them to be normal and acceptable. The only change for the consumer is putting the waste in a specific bin. Which, while an important mindset shift, does not address the whole issue of eliminating waste. Consumption of products in single-use packaging still exists and perpetuates the problem, but simply developing better recycling doesn't change the core issue.

To combat this, TerraCycle has developed another company called Loop that works with major retailers to provide reusable packaging for their products. Similar to the milkman model of years gone by, Loop sends consumers their favorite products in a specially designed bag via UPS, collecting a small deposit from them when they order the products and returning it when the packaging is returned. After collecting the packaging from the consumers home, it is cleaned and refilled—eliminating substantial amounts of packaging in the supply chain.

As we can see, we must learn to surf the waves and pivot as needed to develop a regenerative company.

29 Krishna Thakker, "Report: Private label could be the new online 'challenger brand'," Grocery Dive, June 24, 2019.

REINVENTING OUR WAY TO SUCCESS

Born in Almaty, Kazakhstan under the Soviet Union, Dr. Nadya Zhexembayeva spent much of her early life waiting in lines for food. Suddenly, overnight, the Soviet Union fell, leaving the county with no rules, institutions, or even currency—a state that lasted for several years. From this early challenge, Nadya learned at a young age that change is a reliable constant in life.

Despite these early challenges, Nadya went on to receive a PhD at Case Western Reserve University in Cleveland, Ohio, taught in Slovenia, started a reinvention company that she now leads from Columbus, Ohio, and splits her life between there and Eurasia.

For her, waste isn't just an environmental disaster: it is a tremendous business challenge. In a specific example, she shares with a group of students and environmental professionals:

> For a typical laptop, what would be your guess in the first twelve months how much, out of one hundred percent of things that are mined and used for a laptop, including the laptop itself, how much of it ends up in the landfill in the first twelve months?
>
> What would be your guess? Just give me a number.
>
> Seventy percent a member of the crowd guesses.
>
> Seventy percent goes the landfill? You're an optimist. Somebody else–go higher.

Ninety-five percent another eager audience member shouts.

Ninety-five percent. You're still an optimist. Let's go a little bit higher.

Ninety-nice percent a third ventures with a bit of disbelief.

Ninety-nine. Still a little bit higher. For the average laptop today, it's between 99 and 99.7 percent, but for most laptops it's 99.7 percent.[30]

More than 99 percent of the resources used to create the laptop you likely use every day—maybe even the one on which you are reading or listening to this book—end up in a landfill within the first twelve months of the life of your laptop.

She continues, "If you think about it, it is an environmental disaster. But, if you talk to a business person about it, this is a business disaster because everything we get out of the natural environment costs a lot of money. So, we literally throw away a lot of money. And the thing that we notice from the dynamics of this linear economy is that it's coming to the end. It's very obvious that it's collapsing and coming to the end."[31]

To change this, she argues, it's not enough to continue business as usual and just tack on better recycling and

---

30 Ohio State Environmental Professionals Network, "Sustainability through Reinvention," April 16, 2018, YouTube video, 1:38:10.

31 Ohio State Environmental Professionals Network, "Sustainability through Reinvention," April 16, 2018, YouTube video, 1:38:10.

sustainability initiatives at the end. We must fundamentally change the way we think about business and processes, embedding sustainability in the core of organizations—small and large—and rethink how we manage the scarce resources we have on the planet. We must reinvent business and society with the understanding of these constraints. Much like Kazakhstan, we now have the opportunity to start anew. Are we willing to take it?

WHY SHOULD WE BUILD THINGS FROM TRASH?

- Trash is a significantly under-utilized resource in our society. To put it clearly, we're burying money in landfills, or burning it for power. While that may have worked in the wild west, it seems like a futile use of resources now. However, we have the power to change that!

- Building a business, particularly one with trash as its base, is challenging at best. If we learn to surf the waves, we can surely find ways to make money and reuse trash. It's not easy, but it is worth it.

- We like to give awards to inventors and innovators, but really, we need to recognize the contributions of regenerators. We, as a whole society, need to look at trash and see something not to be sent away; but instead, something that has value and can be used to make something else. That's how we build a circular economy!

PART II

FINDING
REGENERATION

*Humankind has not woven the web of life. We
are but one thread within it. Whatever we
do to the web, we do to ourselves. All things
are bound together. All things connect.*

—CHIEF SEATTLE

CHAPTER 3

MARRY THE PROBLEM

———

I lost my job twice in one year. It sucked.

But I learned a lot.

I work with start-ups and, yes, there is a 90 percent chance that a start-up will fail. Even when you know that going into it, the risk doesn't feel real until you've been handed that pink slip. Then you sit there wondering what to do next. If you love the company's mission—and you likely do love it, or why else would you work long hours for little pay—then it feels like a weird breakup or the loss of a good friend. The losses compound. You lose your team, your friends, and your job—all at once.

Still, bills must be paid, commitments must be kept, and life must be lived, not wallowed in.

I embraced the words of T.F. Hodge, "Head up, heart open. To better days!"[32]

There is no choice but to get up, dust yourself off, swallow your pride, ask for some help, and keep your heart open to any possibilities that come along. In my case, this landed me two great contractor roles and finally a full-time job with a team that I love.

Regenerative entrepreneurs get knocked down time and time again. If you'll indulge my fondness for similes, trying to unwind regulations around trash and recycling is like trying to unwind a yo-yo after a three-year-old has been playing with it—there are knots you have no idea how to unravel. Building supply chains strong enough to scale as your business grows is like trying to build a house on sand—foundations shift, equipment breaks, and the lay of the land is constantly changing.

But somehow you end up with a working yo-yo and a house on stilts. Problems are overcome, innovation occurs, and voila! Things work out.

What makes regenerative entrepreneurs unique is that they see the potential in the tangled yo-yo and the house in the sand. They continue to build even when others would quit and say it's impossible.

---

32 T.F. Hodge, From Within I Rise: Spiritual Triumph Over Death and Conscious Encounters with "The Divine Presence" (American Star Books, 2009).

They ask for help, they find new ways, and they move forward to better days.

"WHEN I SEE A LANDFILL, I SEE A GOLDMINE."

A soft-spoken man, well dressed, and with a heavy Italian accent, says as he stands on stage giving a TEDx talk to students. With a few laughs from the audience, he continues.

Kind and unassuming, Guilio Bonazzi, the founder of the three thousand person textile company Aquafil, begins to tell the story of how his small Italian textile company took on major industry players, created a brand-new supply chain from waste, and has successfully outlasted those same competitors who thought his company was too small to even notice.

He took substantial risks to get there. In 2002, he closed two factories that were burning money, having purchased them after four years of extensive research just two years before. The companies—which produced a raw material, caprolactam, from oil—were intended to provide his larger company and others with the raw material to produce Nylon 6. This is the primary material used to produce carpeting and fishing nets, amongst other textiles. In the wake of September 11 and the oil crises that followed, producing a product that utilized oil as a key raw material became very challenging.

From this failure, he found a bright side. Over the next decade, he worked tirelessly with his team to develop a process to convert Nylon 6 at the end of its life into the basic polymers that it is made of, then produce new Nylon 6 from it. Others were working on the technology as well, but he out-lasted them in a few different ways. He recognized it wasn't just about the break-down and production process, it was also about building a scalable supply chain of Nylon 6 that was ready for recycling. [33]

Ghost nets are estimated to make up 46 percent of the Great Pacific Garbage Patch—a vast alphabet soup of trash swirling around the Pacific—according to a 2018 study by *Scientific Reports*.[34] These nets are made almost entirely from Nylon 6. As a synthetic fiber, they do not disintegrate in the ocean, but rather break down and become smaller pieces of plastic. Worse still, they kill sea life that get caught or weighed down, adding to their destructive power.

In this, though, Giulio saw the bright side. When converted properly, Nylon 6 retains its properties, meaning it can be recycled infinitely in a closed-loop system. The challenge, though, was not just setting up the manufacturing to do so. The challenge was fighting through substantial levels of red tape regarding collecting waste materials, which is highly regulated, even if the intent was to remanufacture them. Still, he persisted despite the challenges, eventually opening an Econyl factory in Slovenia in 2011, the brand name for the regenerated Nylon-6 that Aquafil produces.[35]

---

33   Guilio Bonazzi, "The bright side of waste," TEDxMarrakesh, April 9, 2015, YouTube video, 16:40.

34   Laurent Lebreton et al., "Evidence that the Great Pacific Garbage Patch is rapidly accumulating plastic," *Scientific Reports* 8 (March 2018).

35   Guilio Bonazzi, "The bright side of waste," TEDxMarrakesh, April 9, 2015, YouTube video, 16:40.

To gather enough raw material, Aquafil founded the Healthy Seas Initiative in 2013 in partnership with Star Sock and Ghost Diving. Healthy Seas Initiative's mission is to collect marine waste—particularly ghost nets—and give them new lives, as well as educating the public about marine waste and conservation. To date, Healthy Seas has collected 510 tons of fishing nets, the equivalent weight of four blue whales—the largest mammal on earth.[36]

Econyl has grown substantially, displacing competitors and becoming a leader in the synthetic fiber space. In addition to fishing nets, Econyl now collects used carpeting and converts it back to nylon yarn, converting the nylon while using far less energy than producing raw nylon requires. In fact, according to their own site, "Every 10,000 Tons of ECONYL raw material saves 70,000 barrels of crude oil and avoids 57,100 tons of CO2 equivalent emissions."[37]

Aquafil's journey teaches us that developing a renewable product is not an easy—or fast—process. It took nearly a decade to open the factory capable of converting the fibers, plus several more years to develop the supply chain of waste for conversion. It took creating new organizations—like Healthy Seas—building partnerships with many others in the industry, and resilience in spades to make it all come together. Now, Econyl is hailed as an exemplar in the circular economy, but it didn't happen overnight or without failure. Aquafil

36 "Activity & Communications Report 2019," Healthy Seas Initiative, 2019, 9, accessed September 18, 2020.

37 "Aquafil's regenerated nylon material - ECONYL® contributes to LEED v4 credits," Econyl, accessed September 18, 2020.

continues to push for converting more waste—or gold, as Giulio calls it—to raw materials and products globally.

Aquafil's approach is unique because they out-engineered their larger competitors not with speed or money, but with intentionality and collaboration. They took the time to develop their own supply chain, manufacturing plants, and market to be successful. And they did so while creating long-lasting partnerships with NGOs, their business-to-business customers, and end consumers.

So, when you see a landfill, do you see a goldmine?

BUILD A MOVEMENT, NOT A BUSINESS.

For most budding entrepreneurs, leaders, and high-achievers, there are a few books that stand out as powerful lessons and get passed on from mentor to mentee: *Grit* by Angela Duckworth, *The Hard Thing about Hard Things* by Ben Horowitz, *Rising Strong* by Brene Brown, and *The 4-Hour Work Week* by Tim Ferriss. These demonstrate the mindset required to build a life as an entrepreneur. Perseverance, passion, effort, challenges, and simplification are all things they have heavily researched and provide recommendations on how to overcome challenges and failure. But these lessons all miss something—something each of these leaders has so ingrained in them that they don't even acknowledge.

You see, each of these authors is doing something—they are building.

Not a business, but a movement. And a powerful movement at that. As an entrepreneur, leader, and even just a normal human, we need to stick out hard times, but we also need to know when to pivot; and, most importantly, we need to bring others along with us. Not in a mindless cult-like way, but in an inclusive and thoughtful way.

THIS REALLY IS A MARATHON, NOT A SPRINT

Some businesses grow quickly, but regenerative businesses are rarely in that bunch. If starting a regenerative business were easy, everyone would do it. Time and patience are the best friends of regenerative entrepreneurs. While they certainly still push barriers and move quickly, they understand that building supply chains, changing consumption habits, and developing technology to convert trash to treasure is not a quick process, and they don't give up when they reach base-camp, they continue climbing.

Keep in mind:

- Learn the industry. Regenerative entrepreneurs make their businesses their life's work. They take years to do their research and build the companies they want to see.
- Build the supply chain you need to have—not the one that exists.
- Practice resilience and patience. Big change takes time. "Move fast and break things" doesn't apply here.

WHEN YOU DON'T HAVE THE SUPPLY YOU WANT, BUILD IT

Manufacturing produces two things: a product and waste. While eliminating waste has become a favorite philosophy of factory management—thanks to the Toyota Production System and lean manufacturing— many industries still produce substantial amounts of waste. If the raw materials are cheap, there is little incentive to eliminate waste. As we can see by walking into a variety of discount stores, textile production currently strives for quantity over quality to fuel consumption; so little is done to improve the efficient use of raw materials. According to Pure Waste Textiles website, "Our landfills are bursting with textile waste. Almost three million tons of cotton are wasted in spinning yarns, weaving and cutting fabrics. That's enough material to manufacture three T-shirts for every person on this planet."[38]

When the founders of Pure Waste Textiles, Anders Bengs and Jukka Pesola, set out to find a 100 percent recycled textile manufacturer, they soon found that there wasn't one. No strangers to the sustainable textile industry, the Finns had founded Costo—an accessory company focused on sustainability—but they were looking to expand using recycled fabric. After an intense search, they realized that no company was creating a textile product entirely from waste. Instead of settling for a mostly recycled fabric, they decided to create one.[39]

---

38 "The Challenge," Pure Waste Textiles, accessed September 18, 2020.

39 Anders Bengs, "Purewaste Textiles Introduction," Weedendbee, September 21, 2018, YouTube video, 2:40.

Creating this company was no small task. Three years after deciding to build this company, they finally had a process to break down the waste from other manufacturers and produce new fabric. Now, they have a production facility located in the heart of India's textile manufacturing area, employing two hundred people in a facility built partially from plastic bottles.[40] They separate the scraps they receive from other manufactures by color, break it down, reblend and spin it into new thread, which can then be woven into cotton fabric for t-shirts and other clothing.[41]

Cotton production is very resource intensive. According to their website "Growing only 1 kg (2.2 pounds) of cotton needs over 11000 litres (2900 gallons) of water. That's more than 9 times the amount a person drinks in a year. Making a single cotton T-shirt costs the Earth 2,700 litres of water, not to mention the harmful pollutants the production process releases into the air and soil."[42]

In addition to preventing wasted cotton from ending up in a landfill—by using material that has already been dyed—Pure Waste eliminates that process from their production, which also eliminates a source of pollution due to the chemicals in the dyes.[43]

For Anders, recycling textiles is not the only goal. He states, "Sustainability means everything for us—the tags,

40   "Social Responsibility," Pure Waste Textiles, accessed September 18, 2020.

41   "Production," Pure Waste Textiles, accessed September 18, 2020.

42   "The Challenge," Pure Waste Textiles, accessed September 18, 2020.

43   "Production," Pure Waste Textiles, accessed September 18, 2020.

shipping—everything we do we try to do as sustainable as possible because that's the core business we do."[44]

Indeed the mission of Pure Waste is:

> *"Pure Waste" is our promise to use only materials that would otherwise go to waste. We also wish to challenge the whole perception of waste. Pure Waste is recycling upgraded. Our vision is to recreate the fashion industry, and lead it into a future of sustainability. We want to industrialise textile recycling globally as a common practice.*[45]

Eliminating waste in manufacturing is certainly a noble goal. In many industries, this is becoming far more feasible with the advent of 3D printing and other technologies. With that said, many industries still accept waste as accepted reality. But does that mean we should accept this status quo?

Entrepreneurs are famous for questioning the status quo, and the founders of Pure Waste Textiles are no exception to this. They challenged the status quo—they refused to accept that the industry couldn't be better, and they created the industry they wanted to see, despite the challenges and years it took.

---

44 Anders Bengs, "Pure Waste Textiles Introduction," Weekendbee, September 21, 2018, YouTube video, 2:40.

45 "Company," Pure Waste Textiles, accessed September 18, 2020.

But they aren't doing this to get rich. Anders himself simply loves to be outdoors and spend time with his family. He also loves his work, which he finds meaningful.[46]

Regenerative entrepreneurs aren't focused on the time it will take them to build their business, how much they can sell it for, or what the rewards will be if they are successful. Their companies and mission are their life's work. When they face roadblocks—like regulation in the case of Aquafil, or lacking a supplier in the case of Pure Waste Textiles—they continue to find ways to overcome these obstacles rather than accepting the status quo.

LESSONS FROM MARRY THE PROBLEM:
- Being an entrepreneur is hard. Being a regenerative entrepreneur is in some ways even harder. Prepare for the long haul.
- Regenerative entrepreneurship is dirty and difficult—many entrepreneurs devote their lives to it. Regenerative entrepreneurship is not a get rich quick scheme, but it is fulfilling and meaningful. It takes time and patience to build a company, let alone to also build a network and supply chain to support that company.
- Regenerative entrepreneurs may not make the cover of *Forbes* or become household names like Steve Jobs (let's hope that changes as our society recognizes their influence), but they build these businesses because they feel inspired and cannot resist to build them.

---

46 Anders Bengs, "Purewaste Textiles Introduction," Weedendbee, September 21, 2018, YouTube video, 2:40.

- Building a regenerative business isn't like renting an apartment—it's like getting married and having kids. It's a lifelong commitment.

CHAPTER 4

EMBRACE CREATIVITY

Want to increase your well-being? Get creative! Seriously.

In a 2016 study by researchers in New Zealand and the United States, 658 young adults journaled their emotions over the course of two weeks to measure the amount of time individuals spent in creative pursuits each day and their emotional state. The researchers found very clear results, "Doing creative things today predicts improvements in well-being tomorrow. Full stop."[47]

This research also controlled for personality traits that one might connect with creativity. The results found that personality was not connected to the link between creativity and well-being.

---

47   Jill Suttie, "Doing Something Creative Can Boost Your Well-Being," *Greater Good Magazine*, March 21, 2017.

In essence, making a creative practice part of your daily habit—whether it be cooking, sewing, or creative problem-solving—can lead to more positive emotions and improve overall well-being.

But what does creativity have to do with trash?

A lot actually! Seeing a resource that has potential is half the battle. But finding a new way to use it takes lots of creativity.

We can all be creative, but we have to embrace learning how to be creative. If we aren't born creative, we can cultivate creativity through playfulness and willingness to try and fail while we learn.

Imagine building an entire fort in your living room from boxes, stacked high and taped together, decorated with marker and crayon. There's even a cut-out draw bridge to let in visitors. Sounds like every five-year-old's dream!

Often, young children have this amazing ability to see trash as something special that can be reimagined into an amazing resource. Was there a time when you were young and you repurposed trash into some sort of toy?

In reality, it's just being creative, which is amazing!

CAN WE ACTUALLY PRACTICE BECOMING MORE CREATIVE?

Some people work in professions that are considered creative, such as artists, writers, and designers. Most of us don't, though. Does that mean we can't be creative in our daily lives or even incorporate creativity into our work? Of course not!

- Embrace creativity. Learn to play and accept imperfection. Do things for the joy of doing them, rather than for what we produce.
- Find child-like activities. From doodling in a notebook to playing games to painting or writing, there are plenty of things we can do to let our creative side shine. What did you enjoy as a child and how can you embrace that in life now?
- Get bored. Turn off the phone, computer, and TV and allow boredom to sink in—then get creative with what you do! It sounds unconventional, but it actually is extremely helpful to have some space to allow your mind to create, rather than to bounce back and forth between Google and Spotify.

MY JOURNEY TO BECOMING MORE CREATIVE:
When I was younger, I was actually quite creative. I loved to craft, knit, draw, and experiment with cooking. But as I grew and became more focused on school and achievement, that subsided some. In the world of studying economics at the university level, space for creativity is rare. I completed some projects that allowed for creative thinking and problem-solving, but with pressure to get results and good grades, creating for the sheer joy of doing so remained elusive.

I forgot about creativity for a while after that. I would occasionally have sparks of it where I would go off and write a blog or make a design on my computer, but I lacked any creative habits.

I wish I could say I watched Bob Ross and it inspired me to take up painting or that I had some epiphany while staring at my trash can full of waste, but I didn't. I found my creative side again in an unexpected source—practicing yoga.

I started practicing yoga regularly a few years ago. I immediately began to get some of the results I expected—such as calming my mind and body, and improving my flexibility. What I didn't expect, though, was how it would help me to let go of fear and perfectionism and embrace the joy of learning, trying, and falling.

I have always struggled to learn crow pose, which is where you rest your legs on your triceps and balance on your hands. I can barely hold it now, but when I was first learning I got quite frustrated that I couldn't pick it up quickly. As I have continued to practice, I've realized that it really doesn't matter if I can hold it or not. Sure, it looks cool and it's great if I can. But I have so much fun playing and trying to learn it that it doesn't matter what the result is. I simply enjoy trying. And if I fall—which I do often—I realize that's just part of the process, embrace it, and keep having fun.

I didn't just stop at yoga though. I have started to expand this to other areas of my life. I had a mountain of t-shirts that I had received throughout high school and college—and I only wore three. Some had sentimental value, so I hesitated to donate them. I had an idea. I cut them up and used the sentimental part—often a piece of the back that mentioned an activity I was involved in—to make a keepsake quilt. I turned the leftover t-shirt scraps into t-shirt yarn with which I crocheted a bathroom rug that feels so soft and plush beneath my bare feet. That box of old t-shirts continues to fuel my creativity as I sew a new rag rug. It's a bit of a long project, but since I'm doing it for the sake of enjoying it and not because I need to finish the rug, I'm happy! I use the remaining scraps as dust rags, saving both trees and money.

At this rate, I'll run out of t-shirt scraps before I run out of ideas for them. And that's what creativity is all about!

MAKE CLIMATE COOL AGAIN

Sara Miltenberger, host of the *Make Climate Cool Again* podcast, never planned to be a podcast host or start her own sustainability consulting firm. Instead, she's fallen into it, now helping companies reduce their waste and footprint in creative ways. Her inspiration to do so started at an early age. As a child, she would visit Rhode Island every summer and stay in a house her grandfather had built from a variety of scrap materials. It wasn't only the house that was memorable, it was also near the Newport Mansion—home to the Rockefellers. She learned that in every business Rockefeller started, he always made sure he had a way to sell his trash. For him, there was no such thing as waste—his trash was as much a resource as the products he made. And he made millions, so perhaps he was on to something.

Inspired by entrepreneurship, Sara soon realized there wouldn't be a clear path for her career. As she prepared to graduate from Columbia with an MS in Sustainable Business

Management, she realized she wasn't finding jobs that were the right fit. When she started talking to others in the space, she quickly realized there had to be a way to share the knowledge she was getting from these conversations with others. This inspired her to start a podcast titled *Make Climate Cool Again* because she wanted to make an inclusive space for sustainability. "I want to sit with everyone. It's a picnic. There's no seating chart, sit where you want." Living a more sustainable life is a journey, not a destination, and she wanted to welcome everyone along that journey, no matter where they were. "I think what's amazing about sustainability is you just need to find what works for you and what fits in your lifestyle and be open to those opportunities."

For her, this journey to start her own company has been fraught with challenges, from figuring out how to run a business during Coronavirus to finding great content, but she has learned along the way. One of her biggest hopes is that when people hear the word creative, they imagine themselves because that's how we solve societal problems. In her mind:

> I think when people hear the word creative, they think about artists, they think about musicians, they think about graphic designers or those in visual industries, but I don't think most people would necessarily think of themselves as creative. But I would say that every one of us is problem-solving and engaging in new experiences all the time. If you are thinking about any kind of solution in your life, you're being creative, right? We don't give ourselves enough credit. And I believe the key to sustainability and entrepreneurship in general is really

being that level of intentional and creative about your thought process.

This journey has included getting to spend time with several founders that turn trash to treasure to showcase the issue of trash. For her, trash is not a thing—it's a social construct. We call it trash and deem it worthless because that's what we are taught. But what if we were never taught that? Or, what if we had to carry our trash all around with us, or bury it in our backyard? Would we feel differently about trash then?

At the end of the day, what really matters for sustainability is curiosity and intentionality. To develop a mindset that allows us to see trash differently, we really have to focus on developing a mindset of mindfulness and intention. It takes an ability to see what's been done before and to ask if it is truly the best way, and then to grapple with all of the other ways it could be before selecting the best choice. Creatively solving problems requires recognizing them in the first place, and then being willing to admit that we may need to grow, understand, or change—which is a powerful lesson. For Sara, the main lesson around developing a mindset that embraces sustainability and producing less waste boils down to this:

It's being intentional. If you're aware of all the different things and you've weighed out the decisions and you've done an analysis, when someone asks you why you made the decision, you can say why and lay out the facts. That's what also makes being sustainable different. Sustainable business is hard, because it's hard to confront those issues and think through all of the different options. We really need all the resources and minds that we can to help these companies out when it comes to these decisions, because it is not easy.

Intentionality and creativity go hand in hand. If we accept things as they are—from plastic straws to industrial waste—we never have to think creatively or innovate over how we might be able to creatively reuse, replace, or eliminate those items. The first step is setting an intention to notice what we waste.

It may only be one plastic straw, or one bottle that we recycle instead of throwing it away, but if we all do it together, we can have a powerful impact.

CHANGING AN INDUSTRY TAKES A LOT OF CREATIVITY: I've heard about fast fashion over the past few years. Having lived out of a suitcase for years, I'm pretty used to only buying exactly what I need in terms of clothing. That said, I wanted to learn more about companies that are driving innovation in the clothing and textile industry. As I started to explore their unique solutions, I realized that at their core, they all held one major thing in common—creative problem-solving. Each of the founders of these companies saw a problem, figured out what solved looked like, and then found very creative ways to get there.

What exactly are some of the issues of waste in the fashion industry?

The statistics of textile recycling are appalling. The United States Environmental Protection Agency (EPA) provides the following figures:

> EPA estimated that the generation of textiles in 2017 was 16.9 million tons. This figure represents 6.3 percent of total MSW [Municipal Solid Waste] generation that year. Generation estimates for clothing and footwear were based in part on sales data from the American Apparel and Footwear Association. EPA also found that significant amounts of textiles enter the reuse market, but the amount of reused textiles is not included in the generation estimate. Reused garments and wiper rags enter the waste stream eventually and become a part of MSW generation.

> The recycling rate for all textiles was 15.2 percent in 2017, with 2.6 million tons recycled. Within this figure, EPA estimated that the recycling rate for textiles in clothing and footwear was 13.6 percent based on information from the American Textile Recycling Service. The rate for items such as sheets and pillowcases was 16.3 percent in 2017.

> The total amount of textiles in MSW combusted in 2017 was 3.2 million tons. This was 9.3 percent of MSW combusted with energy recovery. Landfills received 11.2 million tons of MSW textiles in 2017. This was 8 percent of all MSW landfilled."[48]

---

48 "Facts and Figures about Materials, Waste and Recycling, Textiles: Material-Specific Data," United States Environmental Protection Agency, accessed September 19, 2020.

Doing some simple math, 16.9 million tons of textiles divided by the current United States population of 328 million amounts to 103 pounds of textiles produced per person in 2017. Of that, 15 percent, or 15.5 pounds, is recycled. Compare this to 1960, when 1.76 million tons were produced and the US population was 181 million, which amounts to 19.4 pounds of textiles produced per person. We are now able to produce *five times* the number of textiles that we did in 1960, but we somehow cannot manage to recycle that same amount.

As I explored the companies combating fast fashion, I realized that we can learn a lot from them on understanding: what solved looks like, figuring out where the waste really is in the process, and applying it to your whole business—not just creating a product from trash.

Here's a couple of companies that epitomize using creativity successfully:

Girlfriend Collective turns twenty-five plastic bottles into a pair of leggings, so we can sweat and save the planet! They even take their leggings back at the end of their life and recycle them. Their whole mission is based around the idea, "We believe good things come to those who don't waste." They live this out in several ways, including:

> We believe in ethical manufacturing and recycled materials. Because old water bottles and fishing nets look better on you than they do clogging landfills and polluting oceans.

We believe health and wellness come in many shapes and sizes, and that representation matters.

We believe in being transparent, taking care of the people who make your clothes, and never putting our bottom line before what's best for the planet.

We're Girlfriend Collective, and we're glad you're here.[49]

The incredible thing about Girlfriend Collective is that they also take their products back for recycling. Through their Re-Girlfriend program, they take back used activewear to recycle it back into products. They even believe, "The best way to combat textile waste? Buy only what you need, and recycle what you don't."[50]

Talk about commitment to their mission to reduce waste. In their mission to make a better activewear brand that is produced from trash, they have also used their platform to tackle other major issues in the fashion industry including representation, unfit working conditions and pay, and over-consumption. That's serious creativity.

Girlfriend Collective isn't the only company transforming plastic into fashion.

Rothy's creates shoes from plastic bottles. They're unique for a few reasons. They have a signature thread that has been pro-duced from over sixty-six million plastic bottles and marine

---

49 "Who We Are," Girlfriend Collective, accessed September 19, 2020.

50 "ReGirlfriend," Girlfriend Collective, accessed September 20, 2020.

waste, and they 3D print their products to shape, resulting in zero-waste.[51]

This commitment to using waste to create their products is central to their brand. They take this a step further by also embracing a zero-waste manufacturing process, which their website explains:

> *We're especially proud of our 3D knitting technology because it nixes excess fabric. (We fancy ourselves minimalists around here.) By knitting to shape, we eliminate the need to cut small pieces of fabric from larger ones. Little scraps of fabric waste may not seem like a big deal, but add them all together and they become a huge problem.*
>
> *Apparel waste is a global problem. With the rise of fast fashion comes the rising amount of waste in landfills. Not. Good. We create Rothy's to be durable, washable and made to last. And that means less shoes in landfills.*
>
> *Sustainability is knit into our DNA. And that's just the way we like it.*[52]

Textiles aren't the only place where waste can be incorporated into fashion. One unique company, Cinderella Garbage, creates diamonds and jewelry made from garbage. Diamonds

---

51 "Eco Alert: 3D Knitting," Rothy's (blog), April 12, 2019, accessed September 20, 2020.

52 "Eco Alert: 3D Knitting," *Rothy's* (blog), April 12, 2019, accessed September 20, 2020.

are pressurized carbon, so Cinderella Garbage transforms waste, which is also carbon, into modern diamonds by heating and pressurizing it. Their site explains:

> *Once the molecular structure of waste is reduced to its simplest form, what is left resembles a black, slightly translucent and shiny material, which Cinderella Garbage uses to sculpt its "black diamonds." This material is the result of everything that was inorganic in the waste. Cinderella Garbage "diamonds" come from everywhere. Everything that surrounds us is either organic or inorganic: cardboard, plastic, metal, wood, ceramic, water, earth... everything from gift wrapping to a grain of sand!*[53]

Finding creative solutions isn't always easy or obvious. In an interview between the founder of Cinderella Garbage, Kimberlee Clarke, and Sara Miltenberger for the *Make Climate Cool Again* podcast, Kimberlee mentions that the Cinderelite she uses to make her jewelry was actually discovered in a lab for industrial purposes. She saw the potential in it being used in a consumer setting when most were only looking for it to be used as a component in industrial products.[54]

---

53 "About Us," Cinderella Garbage, accessed September 20, 2020.

54 Sara Miltenberger and Kimberlee Clarke, "#25 Trash to Treasure with Cinderella Garbage," April 8, 2020, in *Make Climate Cool Again*, produced by Sara Miltenberger, podcast, 53:00.

KEY LESSONS ON EMBRACING OUR CREATIVE NATURE.

- Creativity is very good for our well-being. We may not always think about it when we are knee deep in work, but making space to be creative is powerful for not only our souls, but also in how we recognize and solve problems.

- Creativity requires a willingness to recognize that things could be different from how they currently are, which involves looking intentionally at what the present situation is, becoming curious about it, and being willing to educate ourselves about it. We have to go off auto-pilot and be willing to see what is really here, which is scary, but also exhilarating!

- Creativity allows us to see what others do not—from gemstones being made from trash to leggings made from water bottles. When we imagine how we might reuse X material, we start to see that there is a world of possibilities ready for us to create them!

CHAPTER 5

BE SCRAPPY

WHAT IS SCRAPPY?

When I hear the word scrappy, I think of someone committed and resourceful, but also showing up ready to get dirty. Embracing the scrappy mentality allows us to find solutions that provide more than just financial benefits—they also benefit our environment and our communities.

YOU'RE GONNA GET DIRTY:

Scrappiness is more than being determined and pushing through—it's getting dirty, dusting off, and trying something new.

I grew up on a small farm in a typical Ohio farming community. Every Labor Day weekend, my family would—in typical, Ohio farming community fashion—hitch up the trailer and haul some of our farm animals to the county fair. We'd sip lemonade and milkshakes while spending all day with our friends. Rain or shine, we would wash and groom our animals and show them off, trying our best to win a blue ribbon. One year, when I was about ten, my older brother decided he wanted to show a cow at the fair, so I of course said I wanted to show a cow, too. I spent the warm summer evenings in the pasture practicing. Imagine a sixty-pound version of me, walking laps around the pasture with my six hundred-pound calf, over and over again. Then came the wonderful day. All of my hard work was about to pay off and I couldn't wait!

I walked into the show ring and walked my cow, Madison, around like I had rehearsed at home. But something in the new environment spooked her and she swung her head. Before I knew it, I landed face down on the ground with a mouth full of dirt. Watching this all happen while standing next to my mother, a family friend leaned over and said, "Better go get ready for tears. She's never showing cows again." My mom grinned, "Just watch. You don't know Kels."

I stood up, smacked my palms against my legs to shake off the dust, and took hold of Madison's halter, determined. I had to be strong and confident. Animals sense when we are nervous, and they react in fear and run. I had to try a new strategy, so I chose to focus and stay clear-headed, as I had done at home a thousand times.

We finished the show. I placed second to last. But I left the ring with my head high, and then I spit the dirt out of my mouth after I left the show ring. It sucked, but I am still glad I didn't run out of the ring.

DON'T BE AFRAID OF A LITTLE RUST:

Rethinking waste is not always the first thing that regenerative founders try. Indeed, some stumble upon it as a business by being creatively involved in their communities. Rust Belt Riders—a hearty Cleveland composting company—was not born out of a need to eliminate waste, but rather by chance when co-founders Daniel and Michael got involved in a community garden and worked with a local farm-to-table restaurant. Deeply intrigued by the idea that consumers were starting to ask and care about where their food comes from, Daniel also began to ponder the missing elements.

"It seemed insufficient, in my mind, like where your food comes from is only half the equation, and nobody was asking the question about where their food ends up going."

Meanwhile, the community farm where they worked—based in urban Cleveland where soil had been eroded and polluted for decades—was struggling to create a nutritious growing environment for local fruits and vegetables. One day, this sparked an idea—what if they use the scraps from the farm-to-table restaurant to create compost for the community garden? Intrigued, and always game for a good DIY project, they mounted a trailer on a mountain bike and began hauling food scraps from the restaurant to the compost heap in the garden.

Every gardener knows that it is nearly impossible to keep good, nitrogen-rich compost a secret. Soon, word spread, and other local restaurants and residents started calling to ask if they would take their food scraps.

Cleveland, like many rust belt cities, may be rife with challenges, but in the right light, it is also ripe with opportunities. Food has always been a central part of Daniel's life. Every night, his family would eat dinner together, instilling in him a love of the community that can be built around food. But it wasn't merely this love of food and community that helped him find his way into regenerative entrepreneurship—it was the ability to reimagine trash as something cool as a child, using scrap wood to make tree forts, and learning from a young age to value and appreciate what you have rather than always seeking something better.

After the initial idea for Rust Belt Riders (RBR) sparked in 2014, the duo scrappily started building out their new project. But their scrappy approach to business didn't stop at a trailer welded to a mountain bike—they hired a few team members but continued working on RBR while working full-time jobs for the first few years. As they looked to expand their products, they realized that it would make sense to sell their compost, but soon they realized that consumers didn't really know what to do with compost. They decided to try and make different products—like potting soil—but doing so requires special machinery that could cost upward of sixty-five thousand dollars. Not to be deterred, they found a way to make their own utilizing materials they already had for about two thousand dollars.

But this isn't to say they are miserly—they take the time to identify their company's needs and wants and find solutions from there. It's a conscious investment in what is required to build a business and support their community.

Daniel credits his upbringing with helping him to see the value of what he has rather than seeking to constantly want more. He brings up a key component of adopting a regenerative mindset, "Being contented and happy with what you have. And ensuring that you treat the resources you do have with the utmost respect and ensure that you get to use them for as long as you can and you care for them as long as you can."

Being comfortable with what you have is a key theme that many regenerative entrepreneurs embrace—they are motivated to enter this field not to get rich but to solve a problem they feel in their lives, and it leads them to greater success.

In many ways, over the first five years of Rust Belt Riders operation, they have become hometown heroes—demonstrating that hard work, resourcefulness, and creativity can bring about amazing results. Indeed, they have been selected to represent Cleveland and Ohio on larger stages, an opportunity they do not take lightly. According to a TechOhio article, "We're working on a paradigm shift so people start thinking about things in a regenerative, cyclical way," said Michael Robinson, co-founder. "We're interested in finding ways to avoid creating waste in the first place. To make it easy for companies, we mimic a lot of the systems they're used to, like recycling or collection services. Once we get our hands on the material, instead of burying it in a landfill, we transform it into something new, like our soil blend tilth."[55]

---

55   Lisa Colbert, "From Waste to Wealth, Rust Belt Riders Transforming Food," *TechOhio*, August 21, 2019.

Valuing underutilized resources is a hallmark of any entre-preneur, but what makes Daniel and Michael unique is their commitment to not only valuing food waste as an underuti-lized resource, but also their value of their city and com-munity as an underutilized resource. "Rust Belt" certainly brings with it a connotation of decay. Indeed, the so-called rust belt was once the shiny epitome of success built by the first wave of industrial entrepreneurs, from Rockefeller to Ford. As time has worn the cities down, many have only seen the decay and waste that has resulted, but those who see the talent and resources in these cities are as important as those who creatively repurpose trash in their businesses.

Rust Belt Riders isn't simply a composting or organic waste company—they are innovators and leaders. They are taking on the idea of what trash really is, turning it on its head, and building a business out of it. They don't have all of the answers, unlimited funds, or state of the art equipment, but they do have an ability to look beyond what others see as trash and reimagine it as something valuable to society, which is vital in today's disposable world.

TURN SCRAP TO STOCK—REMANUFACTURING

Speaking of Cleveland, once a hub for manufacturing, it is now working to regenerate itself as a city. As a Cleveland native, I have wondered, is there a way manufacturing can still play a role in the city's economy? What would it look like? Is it the highly touted advanced manufacturing? Proba-bly. But could there be another way manufacturing could play a role in the city? Perhaps. In thinking about this, I thought back to my days working at Rolls-Royce, and in particular the pristine manufacturing centers we had in Singapore and Virginia. I thought longer about all of the parts we used for everything from airplane engines to cruise ship propellers. But had all of those parts been made of virgin materials? We would overhaul parts and engines, but what if there was something else here that I hadn't noticed at the time, maybe a way to use the parts again? Curious now, I started to dive into a world I recently discovered: remanufacturing.

Remanufacturing isn't recycling or upcycling. It's taking core used components, often called cores, and restoring or manufacturing them again to their original specifications. There are a few companies who do this extremely well:

CATERPILLAR

Having grown up in a rural community, I've seen my fair share of heavy equipment. Caterpillar is a name I know well. Heavy equipment requires substantial amounts of fossil fuel to run, so I was not expecting this brand to be a leader in sustainability. I'm glad to find out I was wrong. Indeed, according to their own website:

> *Caterpillar is a global leader in remanufacturing technology, recycling more than 150 million pounds of end-of-life iron annually. Because we are in the business of returning end-of-life components to same-as-new condition, we reduce waste and minimize the need for raw material to produce new parts. Through remanufacturing, we make one of the greatest contributions*

*to sustainable development—keeping nonrenewable
resources in circulation for multiple lifetimes.* [56]

Remanufacturing is the process of breaking down core components, salvaging parts with any remaining life, and manufacturing them back to the same specifications as new. The process provides like-new performance and reliability, but because the parts are made from previously used materials instead of virgin materials, the cost is significantly reduced. Caterpillar has developed an exchange program, which allows for customers to return a used core and receive a remanufactured one. In doing so, customers are happier because they save money, and then continue to purchase Caterpillar products. Caterpillar benefits because they keep customers using their products longer, increasing the lifetime value of a customer. Environmentally speaking, less raw materials—such as metals and alloys— need to be extracted from the planet, and less energy needs to be invested in turning those raw metals into manufactured parts, reducing emissions.[57]

Caterpillar shows that focusing on long-term value, both for your company and customers, can have significant returns. In finding a creative way to extend the life of their components, they have created a sustainable supply chain, both environmentally and financially.

---

56   "The Benefits of Remanufacturing," Caterpillar, accessed September 21, 2020.

57   "Cat(R) Reman," Caterpillar, accessed September 21, 2020.

NEXTANT AEROSPACE

Parts are not the only thing that can be remanufactured—whole products can be too! Airplanes, particularly small business jets, require a substantial investment in resources, but are often scrapped at the end of their life. Nextant Aerospace is changing that. As the first company to introduce an FAA-certified remanufacturing process for business jets, they have reshaped the business aviation industry. In developing new processes for component repair and testing, they have been recognized as leaders in the industry and received the Laureate Award for doing so.[58]

Nextant highlights that quality and performance do not necessarily need to come at a high cost—but only if we manage resources well. They also show that being scrappy can be applied in any industry—even one as highly regulated as aviation. They serve a variety of high-end customers, including corporations, military, and high net worth individuals, demonstrating that being scrappy doesn't necessarily need to be low quality.

RYPE

Office furniture is another great opportunity for re-manufacturing! Rype Office explains more:

> *Office furniture is perfect for remanufacturing because it uses very long life components – such as steel bases – which are expensive to make from virgin resources. The result can be indistinguishable from new in appearance*

---

58 "Nextant Aerospace," Nextant Aerospace, accessed Sept 21, 2020.

*and performance, yet cost significantly less. Rype Office's
remanufactured furniture is typically half the cost of new,
with no loss of quality.*[59]

Not only are their remanufactured options cheaper, they
are also significantly better for the environment. Rype estimates that their furniture has one-third the environmental
impact of traditional office furniture. Furthermore, because
it's costly to ship furniture a long distance for remanufacturing, Rype is able to create local jobs in their community.[60]

Rype demonstrates that remanufacturing can be a valuable
localized industry—reducing the burden on local landfills,
costs for furniture for companies in their vicinity, and providing valuable jobs. Finding a circular solution takes a little
scrappiness and intentionality, but it can also result in tremendous cost savings and provide considerable environmental and social benefits.

Caterpillar, Nextant, and Rype demonstrate the benefits of
remanufacturing for individual companies, but there is tremendous opportunity for society at large to embrace remanufacturing. While it is a relatively unknown industry, it has
big potential. It's an open field for new entrepreneurs and
large companies to establish a better supply chain, provide
high-quality products at an affordable price, reduce their

---

59 "What is remanufactured office furniture?" *Rype Office* (blog), November
    4, 2018, accessed September 21, 2020.

60 "What is remanufactured office furniture?" *Rype Office* (blog), November
    4, 2018, accessed September 21, 2020.

environmental impact, and even create jobs. According to a 2012 United States International Trade Commission report:

> *The US is the world's largest producer, consumer and exporter of remanufactured products. In its 2012 report, the U.S. International Trade Commission estimated that that the value of US remanufactured production had reached $43 billion by 2011, supporting approximately 180,000 full-time jobs. [Still,] a lack of awareness of remanufacturing and its benefits by dealers, customers and policymakers remains a major obstacle to growth of the industry.*[61]

In focusing on the fundamentals of providing a great quality product to customers, both established companies—like Caterpillar—and emerging ones—like Nextant and Rype—have found ways to create value from trash for their customers, companies, and the environment. These types of solutions are vital as we move toward a new economy, and this mindset is imperative for both new and old companies to embrace.

When we think about being scrappy, remanufacturing might not be the first thing that comes to mind. Extending the life of a product is substantially less resource intensive than producing it new—saving the customer money and the planet from harmful emissions. Being scrappy doesn't mean we settle for something that doesn't serve our needs or breaks

---

61   United States International Trade Commission, *Remanufactured Goods: An Overview of the U.S. and Global Industries, Markets, and Trade,* by Alan Treat, Vincent Hannold, and Jeremy Wise et al., USITC Publication 4356, Washington, DC: 2012, accessed September 21, 2020.

easily—it means we create a system where we focus on producing high-quality products with long-term value.

LESSONS ON BEING SCRAPPY:

- Entrepreneurs are great at finding underutilized potential and bringing it up to full capacity to create value for the world and profits as a result. In letting our imaginations run wild to see the possibilities for recreating new from old, we can start to see new opportunities, and even industries, emerge. But this takes an ability to embrace the dirt and rust that most see and imagine what something could become. It also takes a willingness to engineer a *good enough* solution that does the job rather than waiting until the perfect solution is found.
- Being scrappy is epitomized by the phrase, "Use it up, wear it out, make it do, or do without." It's thinking on your feet, not being afraid to fall, but being ready to jump up, dust off the dirt, and find a way to make it work.
- Old engines, office furniture, and airplane parts may not look like much, but if we take the time to break them down and re-manufacture the components, we can create some amazing, scrappy companies that produce high-quality products at a fraction of the cost—which is good for profits, people, and the planet.

CHAPTER 6

LIVE INTERCONNECTEDLY

WE'RE NOT AT WAR

The Cola Wars helped two companies—Coke and Pepsi. Other brands have built big businesses waging war with their competitors or other stakeholders: Uber went to war with taxi drivers, Airbnb with regulators, Nike with Adidas, FedEx with UPS, the list goes on.[62] But none of the regenerative founders I have ever spoken with or researched has ever said their company is on a mission to beat their competitor. They're not playing a zero sum, us-versus-them game.

---

62 Brad Stone, *The Upstarts: Uber, Airbnb, and the Battle for the New Silicon Valley* (New York: Back Bay Books, 2018). Phil Knight, *Shoe Dog* (New York: Scribner, 2016). Robert E. Spekman, Robert F. Bruner, and Lane Crowder, "Package Wars: FedEx vs. UPS" (case study), *Darden Business School*, February 15, 1996.

We can all win. I know, I sound like a millennial with a trophy case full of participation awards. In all seriousness, playing an us-versus-them game may result in short-term profits, but it can also come with substantial long-term costs. Coke and Pepsi reached a truce years ago. Today, they contend with an even bigger threat: health-conscious consumers wanting nothing to do with their sugary drinks, turning a fight against each other into a fight for the survival of the soda industry.[63]

When we are at war, we are reacting with our fight or flight response, but that's not a healthy way for a human or a company to grow. When we recognize our connection with others, stay curious, and look for collaboration, we grow individually and collectively.

WE'RE ALL ON THE SAME TEAM:

While I lived in Asia, I treated myself to a birthday trip. My itinerary could have included surfing in Bali, adventuring in Bhutan, or maybe even camping in Australia, but instead, I settled on a trip to Kupang.

Where on Earth even is Kupang?

Kupang is located in the far south of Indonesia—a large island known for beautiful marine life and fertile lands. Divided between Indonesia (West Timor) and a separate

---

63 Mallory Russell, "How Pepsi Went from Coke's Greatest Rival to an Also-Ran in the Cola Wars," *Business Insider*, May 12, 2012, accessed September 21, 2020.

country (East Timor or Timor-Leste), the island of Timor has seen its share of joy and pain. Violence ravaged the island from 1975 to 2002 when Timor-Leste was forcibly occupied by the Indonesian military, and to this day both sides face high rates of poverty. Kupang, the capital of West Timor, may not seem like the picture-perfect destination, but once I landed and smelled the earthy, tropical air, I knew I made the right choice.

I had an incredible time! No, I didn't get to lie on the beach or hike up a mountain, but I met some amazing folks and learned a valuable lesson—connection comes when we share kindness and joy. The amazing thing? I learned this from several children under the age of ten who barely spoke English.

Welcome to Roslin Orphanage—a farm called "home" by a few dozen children. Vivacious and upbeat, Roslin serves as a hidden oasis that nurtures both the children and the land around it. First, these children aren't up for adoption—they have a home here at Roslin, adoptive parents, aunties, uncles, and a bunch of adoptive siblings running around to play with. Yes, it can be a little hectic, but what child wouldn't want to live with all of their friends? The air is full of happiness and hope, and the children are often smiling and laughing.

Second, they raise most of their own food on the farm, with the children's help. From banana trees and rice, to tomatoes and catfish, much of the land I see has some sort of food growing on it. This is a great learning opportunity for the children as well!

But what was most surprising to me was not any of these things. It was how connected I felt. How, even though I had just arrived, I immediately felt like one of the family. And how, despite being a little dirty after a trip on a turbo prop plane that was an hour or two late and with my very limited knowledge of the language, we somehow managed to communicate.

Even in my short time there, I could instantly feel how connected we were. Here I was, on the other side of the world from where I was raised, with a new family.

And that's when it hit me—it doesn't matter if I was born in Ohio or West Timor, if I have biological or adoptive parents, what color my skin is, what language I speak, how much money I have, or what passport I have—at the end of the day, we are all humans and we are all interconnected. (To be clear, I do think we have an obligation to ensure that we all have equitable opportunities, which our current systems do not afford to all, but that's another tangent).

Being interconnected means that we recognize each other as brother and sister regardless of our nationality, race, gender, or sexual orientation. Being interconnected means that we feel as deep a connection to our planet as our own mother for the resources she provides us to grow. And being interconnected means we strive to be on one team—the earth team—above all else.

LIVING INTERCONNECTED: THE PATAGONIA STORY:

Yvon Chouinard is not a name that's uttered in most households. Indeed, I wouldn't have recognized it a year ago. Unlike many of the leaders we see today who are motivated by ego and personal legacy, the legacy that Yvon has built stretches far beyond his name. Now a sagely elder in the sustainability and business spheres, he looks on and reflects on the challenges he faced building the billion-dollar brand many of us know today as Patagonia.

A skeptic of business and the man from a young age, Yvon spent much of his youth outdoors: hiking, surfing, and bumming around teaching himself how to make and repair gear for his many adventures. His passion for helping his friends achieve their adventures led to some early success crafting pitons and other climbing equipment while continuing to pursue his own adventures. Eventually, they established a store, added clothing as a product line, and continued growing and scaling to open up several more stores— achieving what many would consider to be great success.[64]

But the path forward was fraught with difficulties. As it began to unfold how devastating consumer culture and textile production were on the environment, Yvon was faced with a new challenge—continue to grow and scale to achieve greater financial success at the cost of the environment which he loved so much, or risk it all to push for innovation and find

---

64   Yvon Chouinard, *Let my people go surfing: the education of a reluctant businessman: including 10 more years of business unusual,* (New York, Penguin Books, 2016).

a way to help the planet while continuing to supply gear to his beloved dirtbag brethren.[65]

No stranger to ascending impossible summits, Yvon set the course for Patagonia on the second path. Declaring the company would find a way to change the sourcing of all its textile materials to less impactful sources: organic cotton and fabrics made from recycled materials. He looked to do whatever it took to clean up their supply chain while maintaining their rigorous quality assurance standards.[66]

Yet, he soon realized that making a cleaner jacket wasn't the only issue he faced in this climb—it was the millions that were thrown away every year, discarded after a season to buy something more fashionable. Never one to follow trends himself, this disposable mindset in the fashion industry left him deeply frustrated. How could he tell people to stop buying his jackets but instead love and repair what they have? How could he convince them their gear was built to last long before the next season of items came out, and it was meant to be loved for a decade or more? And how, if nothing else, could he keep the products he sold from ending up in the dreaded landfill or ocean long before the end of their viable life?[67]

65   Guy Raz and Yvon Chouinard, "Patagonia: Yvon Chouinard," December 14, 2017, in *How I Built This with Guy Raz*, podcast, 27:33.

66   Yvon Chouinard and Greg Dalton, "Yvon Chouinard: Founding Patagonia & Living Simply (Full Program)," Climate One, recorded October 27, 2016, YouTube video, 1:17:36.

67   Yvon Chouinard, *Let my people go surfing: the education of a reluctant businessman: including 10 more years of business unusual,* (New York,

With these questions swirling through his mind, he set off on a new quest to chart a new course for a clothing business—one that repairs, resells, and recycles its own products rather than trying to convince customers to buy a new one for a handsome profit. Creating a system that can extend the life of products and recycle them at the end of it is no easy task. Creating a new system is not only about partnering with the right suppliers, it requires retraining and rethinking the entire company. Store associates need to be trained to complete basic repairs in-house for customers. A warehouse needs to be opened for more in-depth repairs to be completed. Clothing sent back but still in good condition needs to be stored until it is resold. Finally, recycling for each and every individual material needs to be established. The challenges of building the infrastructure for repair and recycling paled in comparison to another challenge: convincing Patagonia's many periphery customers they did not need new clothing, and what they already had was a value far beyond the day they got bored wearing it.[68]

Yvon always worked for his core customers—the dirtbags like him who wore clothes until the end of their life, repaired them countless times, and lived for being outdoors, but not looking like they spent time outside. Nonetheless, he could no longer deny that his beloved company was now a favorite among not only the outdoorsy hippies, but it had become synonymous with quality and it was a staple in closets throughout the world. As much as he wished to deny the

Penguin Books, 2016).

68   Guy Raz and Yvon Chouinard, "Patagonia: Yvon Chouinard," December 14, 2017, in *How I Built This with Guy Raz*, podcast, 27:33.

fact that his jackets were as common in Manhattan as on the Pacific Coast Trail, he knew the company would need to find a way to show urbanites that thrift and caring for their gear was just as important in the concrete jungle as it was in the Amazon.[69]

With this in mind, Patagonia started to lead the way toward thoughtful purchasing, care and repair, reselling gear, and recycling it only at the absolute end of its life. From New York Subway ads stating "You don't need this jacket" to launching Worn Wear, an ecommerce and pop-up store for trading-in and purchasing previously loved Patagonia clothing and gear, the company has taken a stand to ensure that none of its products end up in a landfill and they are lovingly worn for as long as possible. While their work is far from over, living out their motto of "If it's broke, fix it!" has become a key driver of change for Patagonia enthusiasts, and there is no denying they have had a tangible impact on keeping their products in use for as long as possible.[70]

In fact, according to *The Washington Post,* "In its Reno, Nev., service center, Patagonia operates the country's largest outdoor gear-repair shop. During the 2017 fiscal year, it made

69 Yvon Chouinard, *Let my people go surfing: the education of a reluctant businessman: including 10 more years of business unusual,* (New York, Penguin Books, 2016).

70 Yvon Chouinard and Greg Dalton, "Yvon Chouinard: Founding Patagonia & Living Simply (Full Program)," Climate One, recorded October 27, 2016, YouTube video, 1:17:36.

50,295 clothing repairs."[71] That's fifty thousand pieces of clothing that didn't end up in a landfill. And yes, it might mean short-term lost profits where Patagonia could have sold a new t-shirt instead of repairing an old one, but at least Yvon can sleep at night knowing he did not compromise his value of the planet and the people who live on it to make more money.[72]

INTERCONNECTIVITY AND COMPLEXITY ARE INTERTWINED:
Seeing this deep interconnectivity in everything we do also highlights the complexity in our current system, and the way in which it can hinder our ability to find solutions. Patagonia's story highlights how recognizing that we are all interconnected and interdependent can be an asset in developing a company. In recognizing the long-term impact of our businesses, we can design creative solutions for managing waste, and see more connections than we may have noticed at the surface.

Even with this information, however, finding a solution to reducing waste is not as easy as you would think. As a researcher, Dr. Andrew Dent studies and compares the material elements that make up our normal trash. He has found

---

71 Allison Engel, "Inside Patagonia's operation to keep clothing out of land-fills," *The Washington Post*, August 31, 2018.

72 Yvon Chouinard and Greg Dalton, "Yvon Chouinard: Founding Patagonia & Living Simply (Full Program)," Climate One, recorded October 27, 2016, YouTube video, 1:17:36.

that there are many barriers to using waste in products today, which are highlighted below:

1. Getting clean waste. Post-industrial waste, meaning waste coming from manufacturing, is often easier to source than post-consumer waste, because it easier to collect a significant volume, and because there is less risk of it having been contaminated. For instance, he explains, "Let's say I've decided to use a plastic tray that I get takeout in and I then use it to collect the oil when I drain the sump pump in my car. The plastic I'm using is quite porous so it will absorb that oil and then it's contaminated. That's always the challenge."

2. Using all sources of waste. Manufacturing has gotten much leaner throughout the past decades, but there are still waste sources. "However there are plenty of other wastes which are additional to the actual product. So let's say you are producing french fries. There has been an awful lot of washing of the potatoes and you end up with a whole bunch of starchy water that is not really used for anything else now. Now we know we can make that starch into plastics. Of course, I want to make sure that all the real potato waste is going back into french fries or tater tots. But, the starch runoff that would have typically have been used to wash the potatoes as a way of cleaning them could also be used. So yes, I am a great believer in waste."

3. Understanding consumer perceptions. "It's amazing how humans have adapted or have certain levels of appreciation of trash. You have to be very careful about that because there is a company that is producing foam mattresses out of old waste memory foam. Okay, from other mattresses. Currently they can only sell into jails and to

the military, because no one is willing to lay on a mattress that someone else laid on for 10 years. No matter how well you clean it, no one's laying on a secondhand mattress. And so there are certain materials when humans come into contact with them that we think are disgusting, especially now with our current situation. We're getting more and more careful. There are certain materials which lend themselves very well to being used, and certain that don't."

While these barriers are important to understand, a key factor in finding interconnectivity is recognizing the complexity in which it exists. Dr. Dent is also fond of using nature as an analogy. Which, for all of its intrinsic complexity, produces no waste. Our ecosystems are vastly complex, in ways that we are still working to truly understand; but somehow, they manage to overcome this complexity and remain interconnected.

In essence, when we recognize that there are endless types of waste we create all day, from water dirtied by washing our hands to the plastic containers we throw away after dinner. By seeing that our actions impact the world around us and connecting this to our experiences with nature, we can recognize that simple things—such as taking shorter showers—can have a positive impact on the planet.

We have seen how a virus can connect the world, what would happen if instead of fear of a disease, we saw all of the other ways that we could work together to reduce our waste?

KEY LESSONS FROM LIVING INTERCONNECTEDLY

- We are not at war. We are trying to save the planet from ourselves, and the only way we can do that is together. This isn't consumers versus business versus government—we all have a part to play in this. And our actions, no matter how small, have an impact. Put down the weapons, find a way to add value.
- To overcome our idea of waste, we need to first figure out what we really value and stand for.
- For Patagonia, helping others explore and appreciate nature drives them to recognize the connections we all share. For Dr. Dent, understanding complexity and appreciating nature, which has no waste, are equally as important as solving a client's problem.
- When we embrace that our actions interconnect with others—much like the butterfly effect—we can understand that one simple action can be amplified either positively or negatively, and that we have the power to build lives and companies that use waste rather than create it.

CHAPTER 7

FOCUS ON THE VISION

Simon Sinek's book *Start with Why* focuses on *why* building a great company starts with building something to believe in. As he puts it:

> *Great companies don't hire skilled people and motivate them, they hire already motivated people and inspire them. People are either motivated or they are not. Unless you give motivated people something to believe in, something bigger than their job to work toward, they will motivate themselves to find a new job and you'll be stuck with whoever's left.*[73]

Building a regenerative business is hard. It takes years, even decades, for solutions to come full circle. Having a clear reason for tackling the problem you are trying to solve that touches you personally makes this worthwhile. It may be that,

---

73 Simon Sinek, *Start with Why: How Great Leaders Inspire Everyone to Take Action* (London: Penguin, 2013).

like Yvon Chouinard, you find motivation in your adventures to save the environment you dearly love. Or, perhaps you wish to help your local community garden, much like Rust Belt Riders. Whatever the reason for starting a regenerative business, it needs to be clear and motivating for you. Maybe it won't give you butterflies every day, but overall, it should be something you value tremendously. Much like picking a life partner, building a long-term vision for a regenerative business is important for these entrepreneurs.

WHAT IS VISION?

What do we mean by vision? According to Juan Jose De La Torre, Managing Partner at Virtus Digital, "Vision is the vital energy that drives the entrepreneur, the founder, the co-founder and his immediate team. Vision is what makes them *dare*: dare to explore, dare to challenge, dare to insist, dare to keep pushing, dare to have the determination to succeed. Vision is the energy that provides an entrepreneur and its organization with the ability to perform and succeed."[74] For regenerative entrepreneurs, this vision could be anything from reducing a certain kind of waste—say plastic or flip-flops—to eliminating trash altogether. Regardless of what the specific vision is, it drives the regenerative entrepreneur for much of their career. So having a clear vision that motivates the regenerative entrepreneur sets them up for success.

---

74   Juan Jose de la Torre, "Vision: The Driver of Entrepreneurship," Entrepreneur Middle East, January 20, 2016.

FINDING THE VISION

I had originally titled this chapter "Focus on the Mission," but despite the obvious cheesiness that comes with it, it also doesn't feel like it tells the whole story. Companies and organizations often make mission statements that align their goals, who joins their tribe, and provide a goal to work toward. Sometimes, however, these are nicer rhetoric than actual tools. While the mission might be to create the best product, it doesn't fully take into account an essential element—what does the world look like without the problem you seek to solve? For instance, what does the world look like when everyone who needs your product has the best quality that you can produce? Then what?

TerraCycle has a clear vision: a world without waste. This helps them to attract talent, partnerships, investors, and customers whose values align with their vision.

It's not really about the mission that we have then—it's about understanding and sharing the vision of the world we desire to create, and being open to how to get there. We may need to embrace a business model we had never expected, expand our world view, or level up as leaders to create the space for our vision, and that's the whole point.

For most, our vision doesn't come to us randomly in a dream one night. It takes years, sometimes decades, to form, and it is ever expanding and changing. To have vision, we must first be willing to truly see. To seek to understand and to listen, long before we ever speak our own vision.

As we'll see below, finding and focusing on our vision requires a willingness to embrace an ever-evolving process. Regenerative entrepreneurs embrace this fluidity and continue to paddle through the murky waters.

THE PROCESS OF FINDING VISION

I wish I could I say I woke up one day and said, "You know what, I want to write a book about trash!"

No, that's not how this happened. I enjoy writing as a way to think, yes, but I did not plan on trash being my subject. I realized I wanted to write about something sustainability related, but really, trash? Come on, I may be a farm girl, and care about our economy and our environment, but even I'm not *that* granola.

Okay, maybe I am. Just a bit.

We often praise the hero entrepreneurs for being *born* with vision. They knew exactly who they wanted to be and what mark they wanted to leave on the world, they just had to figure out how. We see this in a variety of figures from Steve Jobs, Elon Musk, and even in the stories we show children, like *Hercules* and *The Lion King*.

But sometimes we aren't born with vision. Sometimes, we don't even discover it. Sometimes, it just finds us.

I have always been a big fan of *Mulan*. Why? Because she has no idea that the vision of the future she was raised on—to marry and be a mother—could actually involve her saving the Han Dynasty. (I know it's Disney and not historically accurate, but the point remains.)

She isn't born with vision. She doesn't even discover it. She just kind of falls into it and does her best, which turns out better than anyone would have expected!

Back to this book. I have been thinking and marinating about trash and waste for years, I just hadn't really noticed it as a conscious thought. I saw the effects, and realized I wanted to work to change them. But it wasn't until I watched countless TED Talks, read several books, articles, and not to mention the university thesis I did that looked at social enterprises—some of which were trash based—that I found the vision for this book. Honestly, I'm still finding the vision for this book. And that's okay.

We tend to view vision with a fixed mindset, meaning it remains unchanged. In my mind, some of the best visions lack a specific destination. Mulan did not set out to save China. Instead, visions manifest more like a mountain peak. On clear days, you can see all the way to the top of the peak, but you know how hard the climb to the top will be. The peak might disappear in the midst of clouds, but we still know it stands. If we view our vision with a growth mindset, we know it has a clear peak, even when it is clouded over. Even if we have to move to the other side of the mountain, we still know it's there.

Let's find the mountain top.

EMBRACE THE UGLY

Yesterday, in the middle of this social distancing Covid-19 world, a box full of produce was delivered to my door, not from Amazon or Instacart, but from Hungry Harvest. The sweet potatoes were funky shapes, the Romanesco—a relative of cauliflower—had a few brown spots, and the pears had some scarring, but all were perfectly edible. How, then, did they end up at my door?

According to Hungry Harvest, "Every year, 40 percent of food goes to waste in this country. 20 billion pounds of that is produce that's lost before it ever leaves the farm."[75] More is lost during transport, rejection from grocers, and as surplus supply. But this isn't only an American issue. Globally, the Food and Agricultural Organization of the United Nations estimates that, "The global volume of food wastage is estimated at 1.6 billion tonnes of 'primary product equivalents'."[76] Poverty and malnutrition persist not as a result of a shortage of food globally, but because of the allocation of that food and waste.

How can this be changed? Hungry Harvest tackles this massive issue in a few different ways. First, it gives small scale farmers an outlet for the produce they are unable to sell, or even harvest, due to aesthetic imperfections or surplus, helping them to cover their costs and continue operating. Next, they collect, package, and distribute this produce via a paid subscription to their customers' doorsteps. Finally, some

---

75 "Eliminating Waste," Hungry Harvest, accessed September 23, 2020.

76 "Food Wastage: Key Facts and Figures," Food and Agriculture Organization of the United Nations, accessed September 23, 2020.

of the produce is also sold at a subsidized rate in low-income schools and neighborhoods as part of their Produce in a SNAP program, or donated directly to hunger-solving organizations to fight poverty and food insecurity.

Hungry Harvest takes a multifaceted approach to solving the issues they seek to change—sort of like climbing a mountain from different routes.

To do this, they have reimagined what steps one must take to get produce for their home, and also questioned what requirements consumers truly have. Do they care that apples come in a variety of sizes or that carrots come in funky shapes? Most don't, they just don't have an option to purchase them.

Vanessa who managed Hungry Harvest's Philadelphia Market and now manages the company's Diversity, Equity, Inclusion, and Belonging efforts shared with me this new model that really isn't that new at all. In many ways, grocery stores and fresh produce are a new phenomenon, not the other way around. "I used to always get an orange in my stocking growing up as a child," she explained, "and when I asked my mom why, she said that it was a tradition, her grandmother had done the same." A century ago, oranges and so many other items we now can't imagine our diet without were luxury items, not common goods.

Indeed, since the Great Depression, we have deeply changed what the production and supply of food on our planet looks like. General stores have been replaced by grocers, farm stands by take-out, and home gardens by meal prep delivery kits. Convenience and ease now dominate our fast-paced society. So as new solutions develop, they must support the consumer's desire for ease while providing an equally superior, if not better, product. But how is ugly produce better than what's currently available? In other words, how is trash actually treasure?

First, Hungry Harvest has done an exceptional job solidifying its vision and sharing it to educate its customers. Each box that is received mentions food waste statistics, as do nearly all of their communications. Indeed, they use the idea of *heroes* to describe many of their employees, customers, farmers, and supporters; building on their mission to eliminate food waste and poverty as a heroic, rather than purely economic, pursuit. In doing so, purchasing from them becomes a heroic decision rather than just a convenient one, adding intangible value to the purchasing decision for the consumer, who now values this *trash* as *treasure*.

The key lesson here: find the mountain you want to climb, then plan your route.

According to a CGS *2019 U.S. Consumer Sustainability Survey*, more than two-thirds of the respondents consider sustainability when making a purchase and are willing to pay more for sustainable products.[77] Many brands incorporate sustainability into their product, but what makes Hungry Harvest's approach unique?

---

77 "CGS Survey Reveals 'Sustainability' Is Driving Demand and Customer Loyalty," CGS Incorporated, accessed September 24, 2020.

Hungry Harvest has built a new market segment and reinvented what it means to grocery shop—adding value for customers, suppliers, those impacted by food insecurity, and society as a whole. Finding solutions like this isn't about replacing one product with another, it's about reimagining what the core purpose of an industry is—such as the problem of feeding people, and rebuilding a system that works to change that problem. Many industries, like transportation and retail, are having to reinvent how they can provide value for their customers in our rapidly changing world. Hungry Harvest has utilized this necessity for change while bringing in its value to reduce waste, creating additional societal value in doing so.

FIND DISRUPTIVE MODELS

Several other companies have found ways to solve a customer problem with disruptive solutions.

For instance, as a customer, I recently moved to a new apartment that came furnished with a king-sized bed. A long way from home, and never having had a king-sized bed, I realized I would need a new set of sheets. I thought long and hard about what to do—I could go to a secondhand shop, but there was no guarantee they would have the size I needed, and even if I bought them secondhand, what would I do with them when I moved out? Textile recycling is not readily available in my area, so I was hesitant to buy something that I would eventually have to throw away.

A few hours of research online later, I found a solution. A company that offers sheets essentially on lease. I pay a small monthly fee instead of buying sheets up front, and at the end of the lease, I send them back the sheets, which they resell or upcycle. Since I don't know how long I plan to live in this apartment, this solution works great for me right now. While these sheets are not made from a waste product, the company does take responsibility for upcycling or recycling them at the end of their life—another element of adopting a regenerative mindset.

This moment got me thinking about how many other things in our life we don't really need to own and if there were any more creative models and companies doing something similar.

Renting or leasing items has been known to be quite trendy with millennials for several reasons that benefit both the customer and the company. First, leasing or renting items incentivizes companies to produce durable goods that will last as long as possible, while customers receive a high-quality item at an affordable rate. Plus, customers can send back the item and don't have to worry about end of life recycling. Indeed, renting and leasing have become a popular model in all industries, particularly when the upfront cost to produce an item is high—such as electronics, furniture, party and event items, and even airplane engines. Renting provides a great alternative for items only used sporadically, such as tools and lawn care equipment.

As I continued to explore, I realized I'd seen this in more places. Keeping items in use as long as possible is as important as finding a new place for them when they can no longer be used. Coyuchi takes this into account by offering a take-back program for its bedsheets and textiles—and then resells previously owned sheets that have been cleaned and repaired. It also recycles them when they can no longer be used. [78]

It's also possible for businesses to rent and lease things from each other, reducing the costs of buying new. Kwipped.com helps facilitate this. According to *Forbes,* "Their marketplace has over 4,000 pieces of equipment and $40 million in assets for rent, and the company became profitable after their first year."[79]

Finally, the opportunity of sharing things locally provides a way to reduce consumption and waste. Several apps, such as Peerby, facilitate local sharing for users allowing the 80 percent of things we own but only use once a month to be put to good use![80]

Sharing has taken on a different meaning in the COVID-19 world, but that doesn't necessarily mean the death of the sharing economy. Uber, Lyft, and Airbnb, often hailed as the poster children for the sharing economy, have struggled financially as customers become more concerned about safety and cleanliness over convenience and price. But a bright spot for the sharing economy remains. Instead of large-scale sharing, I believe we will see more grassroots sharing efforts pop up. Pods and bubbles, groups of people

78 "2nd Home Take Back Program," Coyuchi, accessed September 24, 2020.

79 Matt Hunckler, "Kwipped Wants to Be a Disruptive Force in the B2B Equipment Rental Market," Forbes, accessed September 24, 2020.

80 "Handy, sustainable & social," Peerby, accessed October 10, 2020.

who limit their contact to seeing each other so as to limit exposure and the spread of the virus, may still share items among themselves—rather than at a large scale. Communities are also mobilizing and sharing items differently.

For instance, Marta Mainieri founder of *Collaboriamo.org*—a platform offering services for the sharing economy in Italy—points out that, "There is a form of sharing that starts lower down, in communities, and its aim is to respond to real needs...Where there is a community spirit, there has been great resilience."[81] While the service oriented commercial sharing economy may be struggling in some aspects, other areas have a lot of potential! I, for instance, have started using Poshmark—a secondhand clothing app—more to buy clothing essentials that I normally might have gotten in a thrift shop.

KEY LESSONS FROM FOCUSING ON THE VISION:
- Know why you want to solve this particular problem.
- Envision the world with this problem solved and build a business to make that vision come true. Your first idea on how to do so, and possibly even your tenth or hundredth, may fail. Keep working to try and find a solution that creates the better world you envision.
- Don't be afraid of finding innovative models—such as renting, leasing, or sharing—to offer your customers value while still eliminating waste.

---

81 "The future of the sharing economy (if it has one)," Morning FUTURE, accessed September 24, 2020.

PART III

LIVING REGENERATIVELY

I think a hero is any person really intent
on making a better place for all people.

—MAYA ANGELOU

CHAPTER 8

EARLY ON

———

Thirty—the new twenty? Some have said so. The idea that our twenties should be focused on fun and figuring things out may be appealing, but are our twenties *really* made to be thrown away, as our culture might suggest?

I believe nothing is wasted, especially the prime of our youth. Our twenties present opportunities to learn about ourselves in a deep and honest way so we can apply these skills as leaders, doers, parents, aunties, uncles, friends, and partners in the future. This doesn't mean we must dedicate our twenties to churning out productivity. Rather, it means we need to focus and develop instead of hiding in a fake hole of Instagram and Tiger King. But this isn't only my opinion. There's some great research on this as well, such as *The Defining Decade* by Dr. Meg Jay:

> *Our twenties are the defining decade of adulthood. 80 percent of life's most defining moments take place by about age thirty-five. Two-thirds of lifetime wage growth*

happens during the first ten years of a career. More than half of Americans are married or are dating or living with their future partner by age thirty. Personality can change more during our twenties than at any other decade in life. Female fertility peaks at twenty-eight. The brain caps off its last major growth spurt. When it comes to adult development, thirty is not the new twenty. Even if you do nothing, not making choices is a choice all the same. Don't be defined by what you didn't know or didn't do.[82]

In an era of extreme connection via the internet, we also need to learn to determine the noise and the values of our lives. Though difficult amid the endless opportunity for distraction, learning how to manage this and forge our own path is vital in developing as a professional and an entrepreneur.

Jia Tolentino, who built a career on reality TV and criticism of our current culture, takes aim at our obsession with virtual connection, pointing out in *Trick Mirror*:

I have become acutely conscious of the way my brain degrades when I strap it in to receive the full barrage of the internet—these unlimited channels, all constantly reloading with new information: births, deaths, boasts, bombings, jokes, job announcements, ads, warnings, complaints, confessions, and political disasters blitzing our frayed neurons in huge waves of information that

---

82 Meg Jay, *The Defining Decade: Why Your Twenties Matter and How to Make the Most of Them Now* (Edinburgh: Canongate, 2016).

*pummel us and then are instantly replaced. This is an
awful way to live, and it is wearing us down quickly.*[83]

WE CAN USE THESE FORMATIVE YEARS TO GROW INTO OURSELVES, OR TO TRY TO BECOME SOMEONE ELSE

- Focus on learning—not on the degree or the outcomes. As a working professional, and especially as an entrepreneur, you will continuously learn throughout your life. There are plenty of examples of leaders who do not have a formal education in their space, but have become experts in their field by learning on the go.
- Build early and often—Early career is about building a network, transferable skills, and emotional intelligence.
- Lead something—If you have a great idea to start something, do it. But you don't have to quit your day job or college program right away. If you don't start something in your twenties, you're not a failure.
- Learn to be happy as you are—but still work toward bigger goals. Develop some form of meditation or spiritual practice to stay centered in the present.

THERE IS NO PERFECT PATH—HAVE A FEW PLANS IN MIND

I loathe the question *So, where do you see yourself in ten years?* Not because I have no dreams or goals of who I want to be, but because I know they are likely to be adapted as I go along and learn more. I resonate with an idea brought

---

83   Jia Tolentino, *Trick Mirror: Reflections on Self-Delusion* (New York: Random House, 2019).

up in *Designing Your Life* by Bill Burnett and Dave Evans of having a few five-year plans that I'm prototyping and working on, but allow some flexibility in terms of movement as life changes.[84]

With that said, I used my formal education and first few years of my career to set myself up for adaptability. To lead, we need to take care of ourselves first. Do we have the resources to survive? The skills and grit to work through difficult times? Can we think critically to assess what problems we see and work actively to solve them?

I studied Business Economics because it provides a great base to continue learning and think critically about our current world. I also completed a thesis on scaling social enterprises. I graduated and worked in the corporate world for two years. Some days it was a little soul-sucking, but most days I learned from talented leaders and reflected on the type of leader I would (and would not) want to be. I also built savings so I could afford to take a lower paying or riskier opportunity if it came up. I self-reflected on what I truly wanted in life. I wouldn't change it for the world!

Once I saw myself following a more entrepreneurial path, I researched routes to get me there. After many conversations, I joined a fellowship program called Venture for America. I worked for a start-up—which failed nine months later—then moved back home with my parents. I took a contractor role to try out if I wanted to stay closer to home and realized I wasn't

---

84 Bill Burnett and Dave Evans, *Designing Your Life: How to Build a Well-lived, Joyful Life* (New York: Alfred A. Knopf, 2016).

quite ready to move back. I moved to Miami and was let go after six weeks as the Covid-19 pandemic set in. Thankfully, I found another contractor gig that turned into a full-time role, and here I am, writing a book about trash.

But that doesn't tell you how many times I've had to ask myself: *Is this really what I want? Who do I really want to be? Will I be happy? Am I already happy?* Using this time to grow has been a gift—and I cannot help but be grateful for it. I have realized that I value love and integrity, and this extends to all people and the planet. I have learned to value trash.

I can't tell you that I am going to be a millionaire, but I can tell you that I am happy and can rest peacefully each night knowing I am living in alignment with my values, and for me that means I am successful.

SEEK EVERY OPPORTUNITY

Embracing a regenerative mindset isn't solely for business and large organizations. Anyone, in any stage of life, can make a difference by recognizing the impact they have on the world around us. In fact, a group of students creatively found their own solution to a major problem on campus.

At Tulane University in New Orleans, students saw a major problem. Many students attending Tulane come from over five hundred miles away. As a result, few have a way to store their belongings over the summer when they do not live in the dorms. In the past, students might have thrown out everything at the end of the school year, only to have to replace them with new items at the end of summer break—which is costly and wasteful. Additionally, the university has to dispose of the excess waste, so it was damaging for their budget and the environment.

Recognizing this as an issue, a group of several students—including Stuart Rowe, one of the founding members—decided to try and find a way to save and store the items over the summer, and then resell them to students at the beginning of the school year. The first year was a bit challenging, but they made good headway, as Stuart explains:

> We set up collection areas a couple of weeks before move out and received a $10,000 grant from the school to start the program and to pay for truck rentals and offsite storage over the summer. We started collecting used dorm items from just a few dorms and then expanded to more and more as the years went on. Volunteers would work shifts to pick up items from dorms, offload them at a climate-controlled facility, and then organize it all. We would have a sale at the beginning of the year in a big hall on campus and sell the items at a huge discount to make it a no brainer to go to Trash to Treasure before making a trip to Bed, Bath & Beyond or Target. We focused a lot on plastics, furniture, electronics, and clothing, which were the easiest to clean and most-likely to be collected in good or excellent condition after only a year or two of use. As much as possible, we tried to find partners for any items that were more difficult to resell instead of sending unsold items to the trash. For example, we found that animal shelters gladly accepted beat-up towels and blankets and homeless shelters accepted mattresses & pads. At the end of it, we would take the profit

from each sale to cover our costs for the next year, and it was self-sustaining after the first year.

Several students got involved to help, and while it took a lot of work, it ended up being very successful. Stuart served as the volunteer coordinator, meaning he would recruit and train volunteers on their shifts and figure out how to motivate them to join with options such as staying late on campus, moving in early, or meal vouchers. What started with ten volunteers quickly grew to over one hundred.

For him, the experience was one that set him down a path to think more sustainably in his life in general, and he learned a few key lessons.

First, while businesses often incentivize convenience and consumption, it's worthwhile to shift away from this. Doing so requires finding the right tools to help you, using the resources that are already available and devoted to this, and, while it may be sweaty and tiring, it is worthwhile in the end. At the end of the day, Tulane Trash to Treasure prevented twenty-fine thousand pounds of waste from ending up in landfills, so it was worthwhile.

Second, trash is anything that is unusable to that particular person, but it could absolutely have value to someone else. Being aware of that is pivotal to changing our mindset around trash.

Finally, having moved a few times since then, Stuart learned to be resourceful and intentional about his impact: including donating items before he moves and purchasing new items secondhand from thrift stores, offer up, or even extra stuff from friends of friends. While this can take more time to source, it is usually a lot cheaper and better for the environment.

Instead of accepting things as they are, Stuart and the Tulane Treasure to Treasure team chose to forge a new path. It takes work, but it is entirely possible!

THE CAREER WAVE

We often talk about climbing the career ladder. Whenever I hear this phrase, I have this mental picture of a rotting wooden ladder with peeling paint leaning on the side of an abandoned house. I know this is a dramatic reaction to this phrase, but specializing to climb a career ladder seems very risky in today's world. What if a ladder rung is loose or breaks, what if the skills you have built to climb this ladder can be automated away, or what if it makes more sense for your life to stay in one spot rather than to keep climbing? I've also heard the phrase of a career rope swing, which does sound a lot more fun but still misses the flexibility that is required in our current reality.

I think there is something that both of these metaphors miss. A career is not a set object waiting for us to climb or swing on it. It is a living, breathing thing that needs to be able to grow and transform with us.

For this reason, I think of my career not as a ladder, or a swing, but as waves in the ocean.

Waves form far offshore. They make their way toward land, building momentum as they go. As they near the shore, they grow and peak. They finally wash ashore, spreading their powerful tide across the sand.

Our careers are not about becoming leaders or entrepreneurs—those are like the tide of the wave. We must first grow and develop through the ocean before we can become the tide.

But several things must happen for the wave to wash ashore.

For waves to grow, the wave needs a catalyst to start and time and space to grow and develop.

For the wave to peak, it needs to come into contact with a strong base as it nears the shore.

Growing a career starts with small waves far offshore, from which we grow our vision and begin to develop our business, finally washing ashore and spreading our powerful vision.

Unlike the base of a ladder with only one wrung to climb, waves are multifaceted and sometimes a little messy—but that's why it's so much fun to make them!

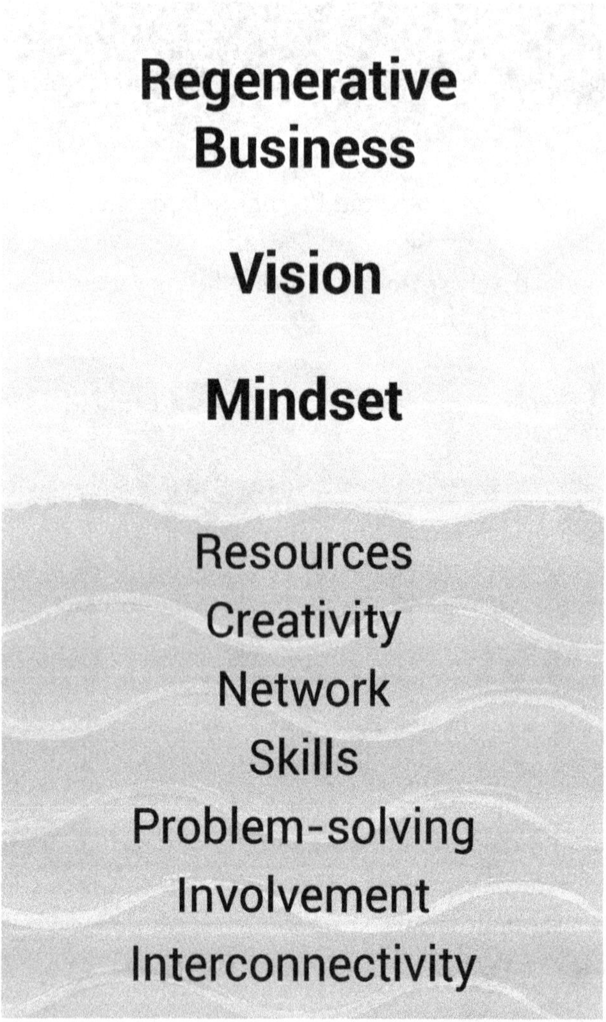

Regenerative Business

Vision

Mindset

Resources
Creativity
Network
Skills
Problem-solving
Involvement
Interconnectivity

Image 1: The Career Wave

THE WAVES IN OUR EARLY CAREER

As small waves and ripples in the ocean grow larger as they near the shore, so too can our skills and mindset in our early career. As students and young professionals, we have a great opportunity to build the mindset of a regenerative entrepreneur and set ourselves up to grow into a beautiful strong wave. Some do start a regenerative business in their early careers, as we see by the founders of Rust Belt Riders and Hungry Harvest, but not all. No matter when we start, we still need to have a strong base.

The early waves in this case are comprised of many things:

1. Resources—We need the basic essentials to survive: a safe place to live, food, and whatever else we need to be healthy humans. This varies by human, but we can't build a regenerative business if we can't take care of ourselves first. For some of us this means having a year's worth of cash to survive, for others this means a job and a side hustle, and some might be able to live in a relative or friend's house rent-free. Whatever the case, making a wave starts with meeting our basic needs.

2. Creativity—Once our basic needs are met to survive, we can start to thrive. Embracing play and creativity can help us to learn more about ourselves and the world around us. As we create, our self-confidence grows and our ability to adapt increases, creating space to develop a vision and lead a regenerative business.

3. Network—We need people in our lives. Some we can share our crazy ideas with and they push us forward, others can support us by introducing us to new people, and

others we can have fun with. A diverse network pushes us to see new perspectives and grows with us.

4. Skills—Hard skills, such as coding, data analysis, and project management, and soft skills, such as emotional intelligence and leadership capability, are important to start building and practicing at a young age. I once heard we should think of skills like a Swiss Army Knife. You may not always know which specific tool or skill you will need, but having a complimentary set to lean on is vital for survival. As a founder, this will also help you to become aware of what you can do yourself and when to bring in an expert to help your business.

5. Problem-solving—How do you use the Swiss Army Knife of skills and creativity together? It may also require calling on your network. Having all of the above traits individually is powerful, but combining them is magical!

6. Involvement—Problems that need solving rarely knock at our front door. We often have to see and experience them, which requires involvement in our communities and our world. If we shelter ourselves with the same group of people, ideas, and routines, we can miss important opportunities to grow and serve as leaders and founders of businesses with a larger purpose. Volunteering, exploring new ideas and places, and spending time with others from a different background expose us to bigger problems.

7. Interconnectivity—When we realize how massive and complex systematic societal problems often are, it's easy to get caught in the mental trap of "I'm just one person, there is no way I can change this, so why should I change if my actions don't matter?" If we only see our actions as individual and not connected to others, we fail to see our ability to influence change and make a difference.

Cultivating a sense of interconnectivity—meaning that what I do impacts others and the planet, and vice versa—we can build an ability to see a space for change. "The Starfish Story" as well as critiques of it provide a great example of this.

CHAPTER 9

CHARTING A NEW COURSE

———

The business of building new products from products tra-ditionally seen as waste remains relatively uncharted water. Regenerative entrepreneurs embrace the challenge. They run—or swim—toward the unknown. This venture into uncharted water parallels the challenges of a career transi-tion, but embracing the unknown can lead to a new, fulfilling career.

Careergasm founder Sarah Vermunt helps people quit jobs they hate and create work they love. Successful transitions rarely happen overnight, so Sarah preaches the importance of being willing to make do without things and the benefits of having "scaffolding and safety-nets." In other words, secure other sources of income and savings to stay afloat while you figure out your new life.[85]

Sometimes, we see career transitions as instantaneous moments during an existential crisis in our lives; but in reality, many career transitions result from intentionally developed projects, sometimes formed through hobbies or projects outside the workplace. In fact, nearly 50 percent of Americans surveyed by Indeed in 2019 reported making a significant career change. Interestingly, the average age of this transition is thirty-nine, pointing to mid-career as a good time to shift to something more fulfilling or with more opportunity to grow. [86]

THE BLUE OCEAN STRATEGY

Render competition irrelevant by creating new markets to capture new demand. In the popular business management book *Blue Ocean Strategy*, authors W. Chan Kim and Renée Mauborgne visualize a large blue ocean of untapped consumer demand. This directly contrasts with red ocean companies that compete viciously against each other.[87] This relates to career transitions and regenerative entrepreneurship. In a literal sense, keeping the oceans blue and clear is a

---

85   Sarah Vermunt, "Considering a Career Change? Here's the Truth About the Messy Middle," Entrepreneur, October 11, 2019.

86   Indeed Editorial Team, "Career Change Report: An Inside Look at Why Workers Shift Gears," Indeed, October 30, 2019.

87   W. Chan Kim and Renée Mauborgne, *Blue Ocean Strategy: How to create uncontested market space and make the competition irrelevant* (Boston: Harvard Business Review Press, 2015).

goal of many regenerative entrepreneurs; but in a figurative sense, most regenerative entrepreneurs create a new market and demand for their products rather than competing heavily with established businesses—so this strategy provides powerful insight.

It also relates to career transitions, which often entail leaving a somewhat crowded red ocean talent pool, where the competition might be other managers or associates, to create a blue ocean career, where you build a unique skill set that adds value and creates a new market and demand. In applying previous skills, you have with new skills you pick up, you create a unique toolbox for yourself. Additionally, by leveraging these skills, you are better able to adapt and withstand the challenges of career changes—and life—in an ever-changing world.

EMBRACE UNCERTAINTY:
Career changers may be quick to associate uncertainty with negative emotions—fear, doubt, loss, etc. What if we changed our view of uncertainty to become more open to the creative possibility that it could lead to? Jonathan Fields is a lawyer turned personal trainer and founder of the wildly popular Good Life Project®. In his book *Uncertainty: Turning Fear and Doubt Into Fuel for Brilliance,* Jonathan shares his personal story of embracing uncertainty in career transitions and entrepreneurship. He had made an intentional career transition from lawyer to personal trainer, taking a substantial pay cut in the process. It just so happens that he also signed a lease to open a yoga studio in New York City on September 10, 2001, the day before the Twin Towers fell, a very difficult time

to start a business in New York City. While these moments were difficult, he learned several valuable lessons on how to use uncertainty to fuel creativity rather than paralysis. First, embracing uncertainty as a root for innovation is a valuable tool in unleashing creativity. Second, developing rituals and practices to help stay anchored—despite uncertainty—helps to allow the mind space for creative problem-solving. Finally, having a supportive group of people around who also embrace uncertainty and creativity is a great way to amplify the process.[88]

Career transitions can be difficult. Learning requires patience and determination, and coupling that with other pressures, such as family or financial challenges, can be even more challenging. When patience grows thin, remember a career transition is a marathon, not a sprint.

Hope for the best, plan for the worst. One of the many reasons side hustles exist is because a lot of new businesses have a risk of failure, or at least not making revenue right away. Regenerative businesses may encounter unexpected hurdles. These can range from trouble getting enough waste to produce a product at scale to facing regulations on the processing of that waste. Because of this, regenerative entrepreneurs should dive in realistically for their financial situation.

As we have seen, regenerative entrepreneurs embrace the challenge of finding a way to use something others don't see

---

88   Jonathan Fields, Uncertainty: Turning Fear and Doubt into Fuel for Brilliance (New York: Portfolio, 2014).

as valuable. Are there things in your life that others don't see the value in? How can you repurpose them so they add value?

WHEN CHANGE HITS BACK

For about a year after I left my corporate job, I asked myself every day if I had made the right choice. Here I was, working longer hours for less money, and at a company on the verge of failure. *What on earth I was thinking?* Then, the company failed, and I had to move back in with my parents to save money and chart a new course. Now I really started wondering if I had made the right decision—I must have been absolutely out of my mind to think this was worth it. A lower salary is one thing, but moving in with your parents is a whole different level of commitment. *By the way, thanks Mom and Dad for taking me in, even if you probably thought I made a crazy choice.*

I sat in my childhood bedroom petting my cat and pondering where my career transition had gone so terribly wrong. *Why couldn't I have been happy with the life I had before and continue doing what I was doing? Why did I have this big idea that I wanted to start my own company? Did I really need to work with a start-up to learn how to start up something of my own?*

Then I realized I had to end my self-doubt and self-judgment. Yes, it had been difficult to watch the failure of the start-up I cared deeply about. Yes, it had been difficult to return to my parents' house and admit I needed their help. And yes, I would do it all again. I had chosen to leave my corporate role because it no longer aligned with my values. I would find the right role in the right company, even if it meant I'd have to create my own. I'd find it, even if it meant moving in with my parents while I figured out what that looked like. And yes, it would all be okay. Eventually.

The most difficult part of changing careers—for me—wasn't the act of learning something new or changing my lifestyle. It was the relentless self-doubt and the constant fear that I'd made the wrong choice. Even if you have dreamed of changing careers for years and worked hard to get to that point, it can still be easy to romanticize the life you had before, particularly when everything falls apart. Finding ways to recognize and embrace this doubt without hindering our ability to move forward is important in any transition.

SEEK OPPORTUNITY EVERYWHERE:
Sometimes problems in our own lives end up being a great catalyst for transitioning to regenerative entrepreneurship. Ciara Imani May, founder of Rebundle— which aims to create a closed loop system for synthetic braid styles—never planned to found a company in the beauty industry. But after having a scalp rash and irritation due to her synthetic style, she began to do more research and discovered the harmful chemicals and plastics that went into making synthetic braid styles.

She realized synthetic braid styles faced two issues that no one was trying to solve together. First, develop synthetic braids that wouldn't cause scalp irritation. Second, find a way to recycle them, since they are normally thrown away. These issues lack easy or fast solutions—they require a deep knowledge of materials science, recycling, and production.

Ciara did not make the transition to being a locks-focused founder immediately. She worked on Rebundle on the side for a year, pitching it at several competitions to get prize money and secure investors, before going full-time.

"Figure out what you know and what you don't," she advises aspiring entrepreneurs. "Then find experts who know."

Transitioning to being a regenerative founder was not easy. She works harder than she ever has, but it has been worthwhile. She also found ways to help manage the risk in the process by laying out her assumptions, testing them, and bringing in experts early.

Ciara demonstrates that we can solve everyday problems by embracing a regenerative mindset. By envisioning a world without waste, she created a meaningful career transition as a result.

NOTHING TO LOSE

Arlan Hamilton is not your average entrepreneur. She built her investment fund, Backstage Capital, while homeless and sleeping on the floor of the San Francisco airport.[89] She invests in underestimated companies built by founders who identify as women, people of color, or LGBTQ.

Why? At thirty-four, Arlan, despite having no experience in entrepreneurship or finance, discovered that less than 10

---

89 Ainsley Harris, "Memo to the Silicon Valley boys' club: Arlan Hamilton has no time for your BS," Fast Company, September 13, 2018.

percent of venture capital goes to companies with minority founders.[90] Venture capital is the funding that helps rapidly growing start-ups—such as Instagram or Uber—start and scale rapidly, driving innovation. The problem with having this funding largely go to companies without a diverse set of founders is that it often misses crucial opportunities to solve problems and innovate. Most venture capitalists (VCs) saw this as a pipeline issue, but Arlan saw it as a lack of resources and an opportunity to change that.[91]

In recognizing that she had nothing to lose, she hit the road to Silicon Valley and pitched every investor she could. In an interview for *Fast Company,* she recalls, "I had no background in finance, but I just saw it as a problem. Maybe it's because I was coming from such a different place that I could recognize it."[92] Finally, one Angel Investor, Susan Kimberlin, took a chance on her and wrote a check for twenty-five thousand dollars in September 2015.[93] Now, five years later, Backstage Capital has invested over seven million dollars in companies built by underrepresented founders. [94]

---

90 Ainsley Harris, "Memo to the Silicon Valley boys' club: Arlan Hamilton has no time for your BS," *Fast Company,* September 13, 2018.

91 Ainsley Harris, "Memo to the Silicon Valley boys' club: Arlan Hamilton has no time for your BS," *Fast Company,* September 13, 2018.

92 Ainsley Harris, "Memo to the Silicon Valley boys' club: Arlan Hamilton has no time for your BS," *Fast Company,* September 13, 2018.

93 Ainsley Harris, "Memo to the Silicon Valley boys' club: Arlan Hamilton has no time for your BS," *Fast Company,* September 13, 2018.

94 "Backstage Capital," Backstage Capital, accessed September 26, 2020.

While not easy or linear, Arlan's journey exhibits her ability to build her vision and business despite her circumstances. This profound message demonstrates that we are capable of leading great change, but only if we dare to reach for it.

FIND AND APPLY:

Career transitions take work. It can feel overwhelming to dive right in, but having a strategy in place helps to soften the hard edges.

Building on the framework we explored in the previous chapter, career transitions are a great opportunity to use the waves we've formed to expand our vision and build a regenerative business. Like a wave peaks as it nears the shore, our vision can expand as we focus and build momentum. When our vision meets the shore and we start our regenerative business, this momentum spreads quickly: like waves spread rapidly across the sand.

If you can find a creative way to repurpose trash, you can find a creative way to repurpose the skills you had from your previous career into your new one. Be scrappy when figuring things out—you never know how it might pay off!

You have nothing to lose. I won't suggest you take undue financial risk. Neither will I advise you to keep doing what you're doing simply because you're afraid to take a risk and do something else.

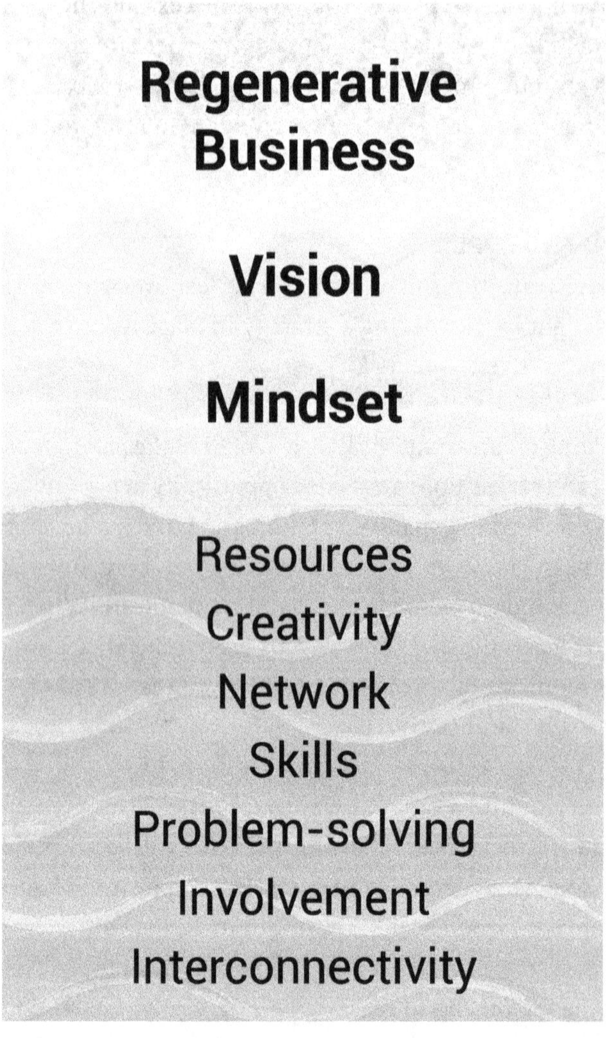

Regenerative Business

Vision

Mindset

Resources
Creativity
Network
Skills
Problem-solving
Involvement
Interconnectivity

Image 2: The Career Wave

KEY LESSONS ON HOW TO APPLY A REGENERATIVE MINDSET IN A CAREER TRANSITION:
Making a career transition to starting or working for a regenerative business is not a quick, or easy process. It's an uncharted territory, and as the leader you become the pioneer making it happen. It can be fun, but there's no map or guidebook to follow. When we embrace this uncertainty, we gain the power to harness it and use it to our advantage.

As hokey as this may sound, one of my favorite things to do during times of doubt is to close my eyes, visualize the doubt, and give it a hug. It's a lot less scary when you see doubt as a scared child in need of a hug rather than an abstract feeling. Doubt becomes much easier to move through when it's lovable and not a brick wall you are continuously trying to climb.

While a variety of people have made successful career transitions despite very challenging circumstances, reducing the risk and creating scaffolding around you helps to make the jump successfully. Like waves need wind and momentum to grow, regenerative founders need supportive systems around them. Close family, friends, and other creatives or entrepreneurs provide moral support and guidance with problem-solving. Have rituals and routines to stay well to continue to nourish yourself and grow.

Regenerative entrepreneurs take on used products, like plastic, that were made to be strong and durable. Like plastic, regenerative entrepreneurs must face career transitions with strength and durability.

CHAPTER 10

LEADING OUR COMMUNITIES

———

The Iroquois Confederacy, the oldest participatory democracy on earth, has a principle that all decisions must be made with the seventh generation in mind.[95] Building on this, how can we bring this mindset that our great-great-great-great-great grandchildren carry an equal say in our community decisions?

Whether you are a community leader by title or by involvement, we all have the ability to shape the future, not just for our future, but also for that of many others.

———

95   "7th Generation Principle," Seven Generations International Foundation, accessed September 28, 2020.

WHAT CAN COMMUNITY LEADERS DO TO SUPPORT REGENERATIVE ENTREPRENEURS?

Waste removal is not only a line on a budget or a household responsibility—it costs us all. From rogue trash littering our neighborhoods to the emissions released during the collection and transportation of waste, every community feels the impact. This local impact does not take into account the harmful gas emissions and land destruction created by the use of landfills, or the monetary value of the wasted resources that end up in them.

Regenerative entrepreneurs need the same community support as regular entrepreneurs, and then some. They must navigate regulations around waste removal, build partnerships to get a supply of reliable recyclable materials, and have the financial resources to discover how to recycle materials that do not currently have a recycling process.

Fortunately, there are some creative ways to do this. The city of Austin, Texas, has set out to achieve zero waste as a community by 2040. To help support this goal, Austin's community leaders developed a pitch competition, [Re]verse Pitch, to allow teams to create products from local waste, such as VHS tapes from the local library. After five weeks of working on their ideas, the winning team received ten thousand dollars as seed funding for their venture.[96] This creatively brings awareness to local waste streams, innovative problem-solving, and supports the development of local regenerative businesses. In doing so, community leaders and

---

96   Bob Gehert, "Helping Austin Reach Zero Waste through Inspiring Entrepreneurship," Waste360, February 24, 2016.

regenerative entrepreneurs promote innovation, resilience, and adaptability in a community—which is vital for the long-term success of the community.

REGENERATIVE COMPANIES HELP THEIR COMMUNITIES:

Regenerative businesses allow entrepreneurs to create their own jobs—even in harsh economic environments. For instance, KI Recycling Company—a Johannesburg based recycling enterprise—started as a way for founder Tshepo Mazubuko to make a living and support his family by collecting waste. After seeing an opportunity in the market to collect and recycle the plastic, Tshepo was able to receive support from Switch Africa Green, a United Nations Environment Program that supports the development of sustainability focused enterprises across several African countries.[97]

Regenerative entrepreneurs help clean the environment around them. As Ryan Anderson writes for *Mongabay News*, on many of today's beaches, washed up flip-flops are a common site. By some estimates, 1.3 trillion flip-flops—few of which are recyclable—float around the ocean. These flipflops create a major environmental crisis for the ocean and an unappealing destination for beach tourists. To combat this, an entrepreneur in Thailand, Dr. Nattapong Nithi-Uthai, spent years looking for a solution. Dr. Nithi-Uthai completed his PhD in the US and was teaching Polymer Science in Thailand when he first learned about this problem from

---

97 "A future in recycling: from street waste collector to entrepreneur," UN Environment Programme, March 11, 2020, accessed September 28, 2020.

a friend—who had asked for his help to upcycle flip-flips that he had collected in beach clean-ups. With the help of his students, he finally found a way to break down the flip-flops into small pieces and reglue them together to make new flip-flops. Inspired by having a place to send washed-up flip-flops, Trash Hero—a beach clean-up organization—has grown to 120 chapters across Southeast Asia, providing other communities with cleaner beaches and inspiring other trashy entrepreneurs. Most importantly, Dr. Nithi-Uthai—who was actually never very concerned about the environment before this project—has now become a serial regenerative entrepreneur, even starting a zero-waste bulk grocery in his own home for members of his community to come and refill containers for supplies.[98]

Regenerative businesses provide long-term value to communities. Yes, it might sound sexy to support a blockchain cryptocurrency internet of things entrepreneur who throws in buzzwords about their company to everyone they meet, but when it comes to solving real problems in communities, regenerative entrepreneurs are a good bet. Why? Because trash removal, much like illness and education, is likely to still be around for at least a decade, if not much longer, creating both stable jobs and tax revenue for local communities. [99]

---

98   Ryan Anderson, "From trash to cash: How a Thai entrepreneur turned used flip-flops into a sustainable business model," *Mongabay News,* January 2, 2020.

99   Robbie Abed, "The World Has an Enormous Trash Problem. Here's What It Can Teach You About Entrepreneurship," Inc.com, accessed September 28, 2020.

Regenerative businesses create jobs. In late 2019, the leader of Aquafil's Slovenia Division, Ediju Krausu, received an award for special achievements in the economy for 2019. AquafilSLO employs nearly nine hundred people, which in a country of two million, is significant.[100] As discussed earlier in this book, Aquafil recycles fishing nets and other items into fabric for use in everything from carpets to swimsuits—building a sustainable business in doing so. Regenerative businesses are not only beneficial for cleaning up the planet—they are also great for the local economy.

HAVING A COMMUNITY IS VITAL AS AN ENTREPRENEUR:

Loneliness is a silent killer for many. A 2017 Harvard study found that the effects of loneliness can be the equivalent of smoking fifteen—yes, fifteen—cigarettes per day.[101] Founders and entrepreneurs often work long or odd hours, and face substantial financial stresses, so having a community of support is vital to overcome the pressures of building a company.

Seeing trash as a resource isn't exactly normal in our society—and swimming against the current is always more difficult than swimming with it. Having others swimming against the current with you, reminding you that the journey will all be worth it, is extremely powerful.

---

100 "Edi Kraus is the recipient of the 2019 Special Achievement Award," Aquafil, November 14, 2019.

101 Charlotte S. Yeh, MD, "The power and prevalence of loneliness," Harvard Health Blog, January 13, 2017.

For me, this is a very personal subject. I work for start-ups and have my own company on the side of my full-time employment, so I know these challenges firsthand. In my life, community support has come in many forms: such as other Venture for America Fellows and local start-up community organizations like Start in CLE in Cleveland or Venture Cafe in Miami. Having this network made failure bearable and helped me to learn several necessary skills for leading and founding a company quickly and effectively. When I am uncertain about how to handle something, need to learn a new skill, or need advice on which technology makes the most sense, this network provides invaluable information to find the best path forward. Without this network around me, I doubt I would have taken the plunge to join the start-ups I did. I doubt I'd be writing this book today. Losing a job was an immense mental burden—losing a job twice even more so—and having a network of cheerleaders who not only empathized with me, but also helped me find a new job, was crucial for survival.

Building a regenerative company is not a solo act—it requires a community supporting it. Financial, regulatory, emotional, and professional support are all necessary for entrepreneurial success.

THINK LOCAL:
One of the reasons why recycling is so challenging is that it usually takes substantial scale to break-even in terms of costs, at least in today's economic system. Additionally, recycling has been highly criticized over the past few years for the fact that many recyclable materials are shipped overseas

for recycling or disposal, where they can be processed for cheaper than they would be domestically.[102]

But is it possible to find local solutions to these issues that would require less transport and still be viable ways to reduce waste locally?

We can start with ourselves. When I was in high school, my mother took up composting. I grew up on a small hobby farm, so we had always fed food scraps to the animals. *Goats love potato and apple peels.* My mom wanted to take it a step further and started a compost bin for most of our organic waste. Even when I moved away to college, I would still keep and bring home items for the compost pile. When I moved further away, this was no longer an option, so I started looking for other solutions. In Miami, I couldn't find any commercial solutions, but I did learn that a few community gardens composted, so I started throwing my organics in the freezer and dropping them off occasionally. I realized that sometimes the best solutions to solving regenerative problems can be local, so I started looking into it more.

The more I explored, the more examples I found of small companies working to make their communities better places by upcycling waste.

First, I discovered the UpCycle Foundation. According to their own site:

---

102 Heidi Lux, "The U.S.'s largest trash hauler has stopped exporting plastic waste to other countries," Good.is, October 28, 2019, accessed September 28, 2019.

The UpCycle Foundation is a registered nonprofit (501c3) focused on creative circular solutions to transform textile waste into valuable raw materials to build a more resourceful world. At UpCycle, we believe that our generation is responsible for creating and maintaining a circular economy. At the forefront of this effort is LOOP! A textile waste management program that recovers textile waste directly from the source to be up-cycled into new materials and products.[103]

The UpCycle Foundation developed a unique local solution and response during the pandemic. They received more than seven thousand misprinted cotton t-shirts in March 2020. Because of Covid-19, the shirts could not be shipped for recycling, so the UpCycle Foundation teamed up with a local seamstress who had been laid-off and started producing face masks.[104]

Another great example of finding a local solution is Alchemy Goods. Based in Seattle, the company started working with local bike shops that provided inner tubes to be upcycled into bags, wallets, etc. The founder, Eli Reich, credits his idea to an unfortunate event:

People say that "necessity is the mother of invention," and that's exactly the way Alchemy Goods got started. My messenger bag got stolen and I needed another one. But the perfect messenger bag eluded me.

---

103 "About Us," UpCycle Foundation, accessed September 28, 2020.

104 "UpCycle Foundation's Response to COVID-19," UpCycle Foundation, March 23, 2020, accessed September 29, 2020.

There were always extra inner tubes lying around my apartment, and I realized that I could probably build the perfect bag out of stuff I already had. The first prototype was born on my home sewing machine. It wasn't perfect, but it was exactly what I needed.

Soon, my friends wanted their own. Then local bike shops caught a glimpse and expressed interest. Each bag improved over the last. Thanks to my friends, demand grew and grew, which led to the founding of Alchemy Goods.

So to whoever it was that stole my bag...you were the inspiration for my imagination. Thank you.[105]

Alchemy Goods has since expanded, now collecting inner-tubes and other items for upcycling through REI nationally. They remain true to their roots, though, and collect as much as they can from local bike shops in Seattle. Their name Alchemy is a play on the medieval alchemist who sought to turn items to gold. Instead of trying to create gold, Alchemy creates items of greater value out of those of lesser value.

Finally, in Nairobi, a plastic recycling business emerged to create fencing for local houses. According to smallstarter. com:

Lorna Rutto resigned her comfortable banking job in 2009 to start EcoPost, a small plastic recycling business. Her business uses plastic waste collected from dumpsites

---

105 "About Alchemy Goods," Alchemy Goods, accessed September 29, 2020.

and garbage cans across Nairobi to manufacture fencing posts. These posts, which are used to fence houses and forest reserves, are becoming a preferred alternative to timber. So far, her innovative business idea has created over 7,000 fencing posts, 500 new jobs, generated more than $150,000 in yearly revenues, saved over 250 acres of forests and removed more than 1,000 tonnes of plastic waste from the environment.[106]

As we see, EcoPost has provided local jobs, reduced waste, and prevented other forms of environmental damage—such as deforestation.

Local solutions provide a powerful opportunity, but they can be difficult to scale. A 2019 study from Nottingham Trent University in the United Kingdom confirmed that upcycling practices are typically small-scale operations, often run in niche businesses. To date, there has been little research on scaling them up as a way to facilitate transition to sustainability.[107] The study also brings out earlier research, citing "Perhaps the biggest challenge for upcycling is summarised by Hirscher et al. (2018), who observe that upcycling necessitates 'systemic changes to the linear fashion scheme, which is currently driven by fast, cheap and low quality production that

---

106 John-Paul Iwuoha, "Lorna Rutto–The innovative entrepreneur who creates wealth and jobs from plastic waste," Smallstarter. June 16, 2013, accessed September 29, 2020.

107 Jagdeep Singh, Kyungeun Sung, Tim Cooper, Katherine West, and Oksana Mont, "Challenges and opportunities for scaling up upcycling businesses – The case of textile and wood upcycling businesses in the UK," *Resources, Conservation, and Recycling* 150, (2019).

fosters easy disposal or replacement, due to the low product value for the customer/user.'"[108] In other words, consumers desire cheap items, which drives cheap production. To change production, consumption must also change.

As it has become more apparent that traditional recycling is not enough to solve the waste crisis, upcycling has become a vital part of the trash to treasure movement. Much of this has been focused on creating local solutions, which can be an important way to solve local problems and build communities and networks to reduce waste in a local geography. While there are challenges in scaling upcycling operations into larger scale solutions, perhaps that isn't the goal? In focusing on building global operations and economies of scale, perhaps we've missed the point of commerce? Business and commerce exist to add value to individual and societal lives, and if some local solutions are able to do so, perhaps that is the end goal for them?

WHAT CAN COMMUNITY LEADERS DO TO EMPOWER REGENERATIVE ENTREPRENEURS?

In the past few chapters, we've explored the idea that building a regenerative business resembles a wave washing up on shore. Community leaders are the wind and water that the wave needs to start and grow. They have the power to

---

108 Jagdeep Singh, Kyungeun Sung, Tim Cooper, Katherine West, and Oksana Mont, "Challenges and opportunities for scaling up upcycling businesses – The case of textile and wood upcycling businesses in the UK," *Resources, Conservation, and Recycling* 150, (2019).

start more waves, help them grow stronger, and harness their energy for good.

Building these waves can take many forms. In the case of Kamikatsu, it took the form of engaging the community in better recycling efforts. The town in Japan now recycles almost everything they consume. This was originally done out of necessity in the early 2000s, when the town could no longer afford to have its waste incinerated or shipped far away—so it began teaching residents how to sort and recycle everything. The key thing we can learn from this is to focus on getting the support of the majority of the community. There were critics of the idea at first, but most residents supported adopting a new, less wasteful, way of life, so community leaders focused on teaching them proper sorting and recycling techniques, and eventually the critics joined in. [109]

From this creative effort, we can also see where it is possible to find ways to involve all walks of life. By including everyone from children to the elderly, creative ideas can flow abundantly. Plus, it helps children learn that regenerative businesses are just as cool, if not cooler, than other businesses.

LESSONS ON REGENERATIVE ENTREPRENEURSHIP FOR COMMUNITY LEADERS:

- Communities need regenerative entrepreneurs—they help reduce the municipal waste removal burden, create

---

109 Justin McCurry, "'No-waste' Japanese village is a peek into carbon-neutral future," *The Guardian*, March 20, 2020.

jobs for community members, and reduce the environmental impact of waste for the community.

- Regenerative entrepreneurs need communities for financial, regulatory, social, and emotional support.
- Community leaders build the communities in which regenerative entrepreneurs can thrive—or die—by their actions.
- Community leaders can create an environment to catalyze regenerative businesses by offering incentives and prizes such as start-up funds. They can provide support and connections for regenerative entrepreneurs to connect within the local networks for mentorship or even trash to be used in their business, and they can create space for non-regenerative entrepreneurs to become involved in ways to reduce waste.

AFTERWARD

———

I do my best to live in accordance with my values. As I set out on the path to publishing, admittedly, I questioned whether the entire endeavor aligned with them. I asked myself, does it make sense to write a book about repurposing waste but then publish it on virgin paper? Would the value of my book's contribution to the world net more than the energy expended to power up the computers, servers, and printers on which the book would be produced? Everything made by man utilizes resources and generates byproduct. How could I make sure I best used those resources and live out *Trash to Treasure* in my own life?

In considering these questions, I looked at the impact of each and made the following decisions:

I chose to work with Kindle Direct Publishing because they publish books on-demand, meaning only books that are ordered are printed. This helps to prevent any excess books being published and recycled if unsold. They are also published in the region they are ordered, reducing transportation emissions. Additionally, I chose the publishing option of printing on 30 percent post-consumer waste recycled material.

To offset the remainder of the paper and production emissions, I donated a tree for every pre-sale book I sold, for a total of 155 trees, which will capture approximately ninety-six metric tons of carbon dioxide over their lifetime.[110]

Closer to home, I used my refurbished computer and phone, which I am doing my best to keep for as long as possible. E-waste is not a widely known issue, but according to DoSomething.org, a website dedicated to motivating positive changes, only about 12.5 percent of e-waste is recycled annually, meaning that Americans throw away approximately sixty million dollars of gold and silver in phones each year. [111]

I have an e-book version, which is estimated to have a lower environmental impact for regular readers.[112]

My sustainable lifestyle has room for improvement. I still occasionally buy coffee in a plastic cup, take long showers, and drive my gas-powered car. And no matter how many keepsake quilts, bath mats, or rag rugs I may make out of my old t-shirts, I suppose I'll still have to throw some things away. But I do my best. We must all do the best we can to change the world around us, even if it's as simple as smiling

---

110 "Leading on Climate Change Solutions," American Forests, accessed October 7, 2020.

111 "11 Facts about E-Waste," Do Something, accessed October 11, 2020.

112 Michael Carpenter, "Books vs ebooks: Protect the environment with this simple decision," The Eco Guide, June 17, 2016.

at a stranger or picking up trash on the beach. There is no perfect environmentalist, nor perfect environmental solution. The journey to living a life of regeneration is, after all, just that—a journey. But you and I are on it together.

Let's do our best!

ACKNOWLEDGMENTS

There are so many ways to say thank you—gracias, merci, granzi, asante, hvala, terima kasih, and tapadh leat—to the ones I love for supporting this book.

To all of my readers, thank you for joining me on this journey and for believing that there is hope to turn trash to treasure.

To my wonderful family, thank you for raising me to be stubborn and determined enough to start and finish this book, and for always being there when the waves get too rough for one to handle alone. To my grandmothers, thank you for teaching me that everything has value and can be reused.

To my incredible Elvis, ti si neverjeten. Thank you for inspiring me to share my writing ability with the world and being with me through the ups and downs of quarantine and writing a book. Skupaj uspevamo.

To my amazing team at FloatMe, thanks for riding the waves of managing work and book with me. I have learned so much from you all!

To Dr. Neil Drobny, thank you for all of your guidance throughout the writing process!

To everyone at Venture for America, Rotary Club of Chardon, Roam, Rolls-Royce, The Ohio State University, University of St. Andrews, Lakeland Community College, Andrews Osborne Academy, Notre Dame Elementary School, and Geauga County 4H, thank you for helping me grow into a concerned citizen and catalyst for the things I care about.

To all my beta readers and early supporters, thank you for believing in this crazy idea long before everyone else did. This book would truly not be here without you!

To all those who made time to be interviewed, thank you for sharing your passion and knowledge with me and so many others along this path.

To all my wonderful friends, thank you for your kindness, wisdom, compassion, and love throughout the years. I would not be who I am today without your support. Thank you for always pushing me to be my best self and for being forgiving when I need to grow.

To Roslin Orphanage, thank you for opening your hearts and becoming a new family in a short amount of time.

To all of those I've met around the world, thank you for opening my eyes to the world of possibilities around us.

To the Geauga County Public Library and Cleveland Public Library, thank you for loaning me countless books that sparked my imagination for this book.

To all the pets I had growing up, thanks for teaching me unconditional love and the value of simple happiness. Bamm-Bamm, I still laugh every time I think of you.

To my partner in crime, thank you for always listening!

Finally, to the amazing teams at the Creator Institute and New Degree Press, thank you for your guidance and effort to make this book into reality. To my editors, Ashley Alvarez, P. Richelle White, and Jeri Ewert, thank you for pushing me to finish this book and for tolerating my despise of deadlines.

To my design team, Gjorgji Pejkovski, Alexander Pavlovich, Nikola Tikoski, and Noemi Bazon, thanks for making my book look beautiful!

TO ALL OF MY BACKERS:

Matthew Alandt
Dane Andrews
Akhil Aniff
Frances Aquino
Kevin Arnall
Joey Bacon
Marina Barboza
Anne Benguerba
Katie Bennett
Sarah Bolte
Andrea Bos

Connie Bowen
Meg Brigman
Perrin Brown
Colette Brown
Michelle Burkett
Andy Bushman
Elishia Candelaresi
Elvis Capalija
Jeff Chen
D'Jae Ch'ng
Kimberlee Clarke

Ryan Cleary
Barry Conrad
Aryn Copeland
Aura cotofan
Nathan Crooks
Emily Cubbage
Taylor Davis
Maria de Caris
Serena Deutch
Richard Doringo
Gabba Dowling
Lauren Dunaway
Rachel Dunnam
Eric Erkis
Bob Faehnle
Hannah Falberg
Hana Feiner
Alisa Feng
Danna Frazier
Joe Galt
Alfonso Gillette
Hannah Goddard
Elianna Goldstein
Jennifer Gomez
Jordyn Grant
Henry Grierson
John Harris Alexander
Rob Hatfield
Jessica Hazel-Draganic
Terry Hegner
Michael Hsun
Vaughn Hunt

Donald Huston
Samreen Islam
Benjamin Ko
Eric Koester
Julia kortberg
Michelle Kowalski
Rachel Krasnick
James Kubitz
Shannon Langdon
Lynn Langdon Mays
Michael Lee
Veronica Leigh Head
Mordi Linfield
Matt Lopez
Ruidi Lu
Elizabeth Luckman
Yiannoula Mavroidis
Lorie McCoy
Laura McIlvain
Briana Mele
Daniel Miller
Brandon Mitchell
Liberty Mosher
Marc Mouhadeb
Carrie Murphy
Rahul Narain
Amy Nelson
Kane Ng
Kevin & Nancy O'Reilly
Luisa Paganini
Vikram Patel
Molly Peralta

Vincent Po
Annjana Ramesh
Garrett Ransom
Kristy Reed
Jonathan Restivo
Christopher Rios-Villalobos
Alister Riviere
Jenny Rukenbrod
Mary Beth & Ed Rumburg
Jeanne Rumburg
Josh Sanchez
Claire Shaw
Michelle Sims
Patrick Sours
Jonny Sywulak

Serena Thomas
Nick Urig
Terence Urig
Tyler Urig
Susan Urig
Andre Ward
Stephen Weaver
Maggie Wehri
Robert Wernke
Tally Wolff
Aaron & Anuja
Courtney
Koko
Jonathan & Kim

APPENDIX

INTRODUCTION

Feeding America. "How We Fight Food Waste in the US." Accessed September 12, 2020. https://www.feedingamerica.org/our-work/our-approach/reduce-food-waste.

Humes, Edward. *Garbology: Our Dirty Love Affair with Trash*. New York: Avery, 2012. Kindle.

Simmons, Ann M. "The world's trash crisis, and why many Americans are oblivious." *Los Angeles Times,* April 22, 2016. https://www.latimes.com/world/global-development/la-fg-global-trash-20160422-20160421-snap-htmlstory.html.

U.S. Department of Agriculture. "Food Waste FAQs." Accessed September 12, 2020. https://www.usda.gov/foodwaste/faqs.

CHAPTER 1

Brickman, P., D. Coates, and R. Janoff-Bulman, "Lottery winners and accident victims: is happiness relative?" *Journal of Person-*

ality and Social Psychology 36, no. 8, (1978): 917–927. https://doi.org/10.1037//0022-3514.36.8.917.

CBS News. "How a great sale affects your brain." *CBS News,* December 15, 2013. Accessed September 12, 2020. https://www.cbsnews.com/news/how-a-great-sale-affects-your-brain/.

Gomes, Robin. "Pope: Economics without ethics leads to 'throwaway' culture." *Vatican News.* November 11, 2019. https://www.vaticannews.va/en/pope/news/2019-11/pope-francis-economy-inclusive-capitalism.html.

Humes, Edward. *Garbology: Our Dirty Love Affair with Trash.* New York: Avery, 2012. Kindle.

Iannucci, Lisa. "Where Does the Garbage Go?" The Cooperator New York. September 2006. Accessed September 13, 2020. https://cooperator.com/article/where-does-the-garbage-go/full.

Jacobsen, Rowan. "An Ocean Plastics Field Trip for Corporate Executives." *Outside,* August 8, 2019. https://www.outsideonline.com/2400590/ocean-plastic-pollution-soulbuffalo.

Kumar, Amit, Matthew A. Killingsworth, and Thomas Gilovich. "Spending on doing promotes more moment-to-moment happiness than spending on having." *Journal of Experimental Social Psychology* 99, May 2020. https://www.sciencedirect.com/science/article/abs/pii/S0022103119305256?via%3Dihub#!

MacArthur, Ellen. "Why our throwaway culture has to end." *National Geographic,* June 6, 2018. https://www.nationalgeographic.co.uk/environment-and-conservation/2018/06/why-our-throwaway-culture-has-end.

Parker, Dianna. "Why is plastic marine debris so common?" Produced by Kurt Mann for Ocean Today. Video, 2:22. Accessed September 14, 2020. https://oceantoday.noaa.gov/trashtalk_plastics/welcome.html.

PBS: Public Broadcasting Service. "The Rise of American Consumerism." Accessed September 12, 2020. https://www.pbs.org/wgbh/americanexperience/features/tupperware-consumer/.

Perry, Mark J. "New US homes today are 1,000 square feet larger than in 1973 and living space per person has nearly doubled." *American Enterprise Institute* (blog), June 5, 2016. Accessed September 12, 2020. https://www.aei.org/carpe-diem/new-us-homes-today-are-1000-square-feet-larger-than-in-1973-and-living-space-per-person-has-nearly-doubled/.

"Talking trash." *The Economist* Technology Quarterly. June 2, 2012. https://www.economist.com/technology-quarterly/2012/06/02/talking-trash.

Taylor, Duncan M. and David Segal. "Healing Ourselves and Healing the World: Consumerism and the Culture of Addiction." *Journal of Future Studies* 19 (2015): 77–86. https://bestfutures.org/wp-content/uploads/2018/05/Taylor-Segal_Healing-Ourselves-and-Healing-the-World.pdf.

"Throwaway Living." *Life.* August 1955.

United States Environmental Protection Agency. "National Overview: Facts and Figures on Materials, Wastes and Recycling." Accessed September 19, 2020. https://www.epa.gov/facts-and-figures-about-materials-waste-and-recycling/national-overview-facts-and-figures-materials.

University of Kansas. "Throwaway culture can include friendships, researcher says." *ScienceDaily*. Accessed September 14, 2020. www.sciencedaily.com/releases/2016/02/160222144332.htm.

Walsh, Nick Paton, Ingrid Formanek, Jackson Loo, and Mark Phillips. "Plastic Island: How our throwaway culture is turning paradise into a graveyard." *CNN*. Accessed September 14, 2020. https://www.cnn.com/interactive/2016/12/world/midway-plastic-island/.

Zimmerman, Elizabeth A. "How We Became a Throw-away Society." Our Better Nature (blog). April 4, 2008. http://www.ourbetternature.org/throwaway.htm

CHAPTER 2

Bhasin, Kim. "The Incredible Story of How TerraCycle CEO Tom Szaky Became A Garbage Mogul." *Business Insider*. August 29, 2011. https://www.businessinsider.com/exclusive-tom-szaky-TerraCycle-interview-2011-8.

Crunchbase. "TerraCycle." Accessed September 15, 2020. https://www.crunchbase.com/organization/TerraCycle.

Decker, Ryan, John Haltiwanger, Ron Jarmin, and Javier Miranda, "The Role of Entrepreneurship in US Job Creation and Economic Dynamism," *Journal of Economic Perspectives* 28, no. 3 (2014): 3–24. http://econweb.umd.edu/~haltiwan/JEP_DHJM. pdf.

"Ocean Pollution Doesn't Wash Away'." TerraCycle Blog (blog). November 26, 2019, accessed September 15, 2020. https://blog.terraCycle.com/2019/11/26/ocean-pollution-doesnt-wash-away/.

Ohio State Environmental Professionals Network. "Sustainability through Reinvention." April 16, 2018. YouTube video, 1:38:10. https://www.youtube.com/watch?v=KB3r1NjhvsA.

Start Engine. "TerraCycle." Accessed October 10, 2020. https://www.startengine.com/terracycle.

Thakker, Krishna. "Report: Private label could be the new online 'challenger brand'." Grocery Dive. June 24, 2019. https://www.grocerydive.com/news/report-private-label-could-be-the-new-online-challenger-brand/557460/.

Workman, Megan (ed.). "SEC qualifies $25 million Regulation A capital raise for TerraCycle US." *Recycling Today,* January 18, 2018. https://www.recyclingtoday.com/article/sec-regulation-a-capital-TerraCycle-invest/.

Yang, Andrew. *Smart People Should Build Things.* New York: HarperCollins, 2014. Kindle.

CHAPTER 3

"Activity & Communications Report 2019." Healthy Seas Initiative. 2019, 9. Accessed September 18, 2020. https://healthyseas.org/assets/uploads/2020/01/Healthy-Seas-Report-2019.pdf.

"Aquafil's regenerated nylon material – ECONYL® contributes to LEED v4 credits," Econyl, accessed September 18, 2020. https://www.econyl.com/press/aquafils-regenerated-nylon-material-econyl-contributes-to-leed-v4-credits/.

Bengs, Anders. "Purewaste Textiles Introduction." Weedendbee. September 21, 2018. YouTube video, 2:40. https://www.youtube.com/watch?v=4CUH6duPEMc.

Bonazzi, Guilio. "The bright side of waste." TEDxMarrakesh. April 9, 2015. YouTube video, 16:40. https://www.youtube.com/watch?v=fR57-CSRJfM.

"Company." Pure Waste Textiles. Accessed September 18, 2020. https://www.purewastetextiles.com/purewastetextiles/.

Hodge, T.F. *From Within I Rise: Spiritual Triumph Over Death and Conscious Encounters with "The Divine Presence."* American Star Books, 2009.

Lebreton, Laurent, Boyan Slat, Francesco Ferrari, Bruno Sainte-Rose, J Aitken, R Marthouse, Sara Hajbane, et al. "Evidence that the Great Pacific Garbage Patch is rapidly accumulating plastic." Scientific Reports 8 (March 2018). https://www.researchgate.net/publication/323943462_Evidence_that_the_Great_Pacific_Garbage_Patch_is_rapidly_accumulating_plastic.

"Production." Pure Waste Textiles. Accessed September 18, 2020. https://www.purewastetextiles.com/.

"Social Responsibility." Pure Waste Textiles. Accessed September 18, 2020. http://www.purewastetextiles.com/social-responsibility-page/.

"The Challenge." Pure Waste Textiles. Accessed September 18, 2020. http://www.purewastetextiles.com/the-problem-page/.

CHAPTER 4

Cinderella Garbage. "About Us." Accessed September 20, 2020. https://www.cinderellagarbage.com/pages/about-us.

Girlfriend Collective. "ReGirlfriend." Accessed September 20, 2020. https://www.girlfriend.com/pages/regirlfriend.

Girlfriend Collective. "Who We Are." Accessed September 19, 2020. https://www.girlfriend.com/pages/our-story.

Miltenberger, Sara and Kimberlee Clarke. "#25 Trash to Treasure with Cinderella Garbage." April 8, 2020. In Make Climate Cool Again. Produced by Sara Miltenberger. Podcast, 53:00. https://anchor.fm/makeclimatecool/episodes/25-Trash-to-Treasure-with-Cinderella-Garbage-echpbj/a-a1sq059.

Rothy's (blog). "Eco Alert: 3D Knitting." April 12, 2019. Accessed September 20, 2020. https://rothys.com/blog/sustainability/articles/eco-alert-3d-knitting.

Rothy's. "Sustainability." Accessed September 20, 2020. https://
rothys.com/sustainability.

Suttie, Jill. "Doing Something Creative Can Boost Your Well-Being."
Greater Good Magazine, March 21, 2017. https://greatergood.
berkeley.edu/article/item/doing_something_creative_can_
boost_your_well_being.

United States Environmental Protection Agency. "Facts and Figures about Materials, Waste and Recycling, Textiles: Material-Specific Data." Accessed September 19, 2020. https://www.
epa.gov/facts-and-figures-about-materials-waste-and-recy-
cling/textiles-material-specific-data.

CHAPTER 5

Caterpillar. "Cat(R) Reman." Accessed September 21, 2020. https://
www.caterpillar.com/en/brands/cat-reman.html.

Caterpillar. "The Benefits of Remanufacturing." Accessed September 21, 2020. https://www.caterpillar.com/en/company/
sustainability/remanufacturing/benefits.html.

Colbert, Lisa. "From Waste to Wealth, Rust Belt Riders Transforming Food." TechOhio. August 21, 2019. https://weare.techohio.
ohio.gov/2019/08/21/from-waste-to-wealth-rust-belt-riders-
transforming-food.

Nextant Aerospace. "Nextant Aerospace." Accessed Sept 21, 2020.
https://www.nextantaerospace.com/.

Rype Office (blog). "What is remanufactured office furniture?" November 4, 2018. Accessed September 21, 2020. https://www. rypeoffice.com/what-is-remanufactured-office-furniture/.

United States International Trade Commission. *Remanufactured Goods: An Overview of the U.S. and Global Industries, Markets, and Trade.* By Alan Treat, Vincent Hannold, and Jeremy Wise et al., USITC Publication 4356. Washington, D.C.: 2012. Accessed September 21, 2020. https://www.usitc.gov/publications/332/pub4356.pdf.

CHAPTER 6

Chouinard, Yvon. *Let my people go surfing: the education of a reluctant businessman: including 10 more years of business unusual.* New York: Penguin Books, 2016.

Chouinard, Yvon and Greg Dalton. "Yvon Chouinard: Founding Patagonia & Living Simply (Full Program)." Climate One. Recorded October 27, 2016. YouTube video, 1:17:36. https://www. youtube.com/watch?v=SP52ysowApg&feature=youtu.be.

Engel, Allison. "Inside Patagonia's operation to keep clothing out of landfills." *The Washington Post.* August 31, 2018. https://www. washingtonpost.com/business/inside-patagonias-operation-to-keep-you-from-buying-new-gear/2018/08/31/d3d1fab4-ac8c-11e8-b1da-ff7faa680710_story.html.

Knight, Phil. *Shoe Dog.* New York: Scribner, 2016.

Raz, Guy and Yvon Chouinard. "Patagonia: Yvon Chouinard." December 14, 2017. In How I Built This with Guy Raz. Podcast.

27:33. https://www.stitcher.com/podcast/national-public-radio/how-i-built-this/e/patagonia-yvon-chouinard-48508362.

Russell, Mallory. "How Pepsi Went from Coke's Greatest Rival to an Also-Ran in the Cola Wars." *Business Insider.* May 12, 2012. Accessed September 21, 2020. https://www.businessinsider.com/how-pepsi-lost-cola-war-against-coke-2012-5.

Spekman, Robert E., Robert F. Bruner, and Lane Crowder. "Package Wars: FedEx vs. UPS" (case study). Darden Business School. February 15, 1996. https://store.hbr.org/product/package-war-fedex-vs-ups/UV0015.

Stone, Brad. *The Upstarts: Uber, Airbnb, and the Battle for the New Silicon Valley.* New York: Back Bay Books, 2018.

CHAPTER 7

CGS Incorporated. "CGS Survey Reveals 'Sustainability' Is Driving Demand and Customer Loyalty." Accessed September 24, 2020. https://www.cgsinc.com/en/infographics/CGS-Survey-Reveals-Sustainability-Is-Driving-Demand-and-Customer-Loyalty.

Coyuchi. "2nd Home Take Back Program." Accessed September 24, 2020. https://www.coyuchi.com/secondhome.

De la Torre, Juan Jose. "Vision: The Driver of Entrepreneurship". *Entrepreneur Middle East.* January 20, 2016. https://www.entrepreneur.com/article/269757.

Food and Agriculture Organization of the United Nations. "Food Wastage: Key Facts and Figures." Accessed September 23, 2020. http://www.fao.org/news/story/en/item/196402/.

Hunckler, Matt. "Kwipped Wants to Be a Disruptive Force in the B2B Equipment Rental Market." *Forbes*. Accessed September 24, 2020. https://www.forbes.com/sites/matthunckler/2016/09/16/kwipped-wants-to-be-a-disruptive-force-in-the-b2b-equipment-rental-market/#405af816d08a.

Hungry Harvest. "Eliminating Waste." Accessed September 23, 2020. https://www.hungryharvest.net/eliminating-food-waste.

Jaisoor, N.S. "The Sharing Economy Is Good for the Environment. Here's Why." Accessed September 24, 2020. https://medium.com/nomobo/the-sharing-economy-is-good-for-the-environment-heres-why-db37214215f7.

Sinek, Simon. *Start with Why: How Great Leaders Inspire Everyone to Take Action*. London: Penguin, 2013.

"The future of the sharing economy (if it has one)." *Morning FUTURE*. Accessed September 24, 2020. https://www.morningfuture.com/en/article/2020/07/17/sharing-economy-crisis-marta-mainieri/968/.

CHAPTER 8

Burnett, Bill and Dave Evans. *Designing Your Life: How to Build a Well-lived, Joyful Life*. New York: Alfred A. Knopf. 2016.

Jay, Meg. *The Defining Decade: Why Your Twenties Matter and How to Make the Most of Them Now.* Edinburgh: Canongate. 2016.

Tolentino, Jia. *Trick Mirror: reflections on self-delusion.* New York: Random House. 2019.

CHAPTER 9

Backstage Capital. "Backstage Capital." Accessed September 26, 2020. https://backstagecapital.com/.

Chan Kim, W and Renée Mauborgne. *Blue Ocean Strategy: How to create uncontested market space and make the competition irrelevant.* Boston: Harvard Business Review Press, 2015.

Harris, Ainsley. "Memo to the Silicon Valley boys' club: Arlan Hamilton has no time for your BS." *Fast Company.* September 13, 2018. https://www.fastcompany.com/90227793/backstage-capitals-arlan-hamilton-brings-diversity-to-venture-capital.

Fields, Jonathan. *Uncertainty: Turning Fear and Doubt into Fuel for Brilliance.* New York: Portfolio, 2014.

Indeed Editorial Team. "Career Change Report: An Inside Look at Why Workers Shift Gears." Indeed. October 30, 2019. https://www.indeed.com/lead/career-change.

Vermunt, Sarah. "Considering a Career Change? Here's the Truth About the Messy Middle." *Entrepreneur.* October 11, 2019. https://www.entrepreneur.com/article/340608.

CHAPTER 10

Abed, Robbie. "The World Has an Enormous Trash Problem. Here's What It Can Teach You About Entrepreneurship." Inc. com. Accessed September 28, 2020. https://www.inc.com/robbie-abed/the-world-has-an-enormous-trash-problem-heres-what-it-can-teach-you-about-entrepreneurship.html.

Alchemy Goods. "About Alchemy Goods." Alchemy Goods. Accessed September 29, 2020. https://www.alchemygoods.com/pages/about-us.

Anderson, Ryan. "From trash to cash: How a Thai entrepreneur turned used flip-flops into a sustainable business model." *Mongabay News*. January 2, 2020. https://news.mongabay.com/2020/01/from-trash-to-cash-how-a-thai-entrepreneur-turned-used-flip-flops-into-a-sustainable-business-model/.

Aquafil. "Edi Kraus is the recipient of the 2019 Special Achievement Award." November 14, 2019. https://www.aquafil.com/localnews/edi-kraus-je-prejemnik-nagrade-za-posebne-dosezke-v-gospodarstvu-2019/.

Gehert, Bob. "Helping Austin Reach Zero Waste through Inspiring Entrepreneurship." Waste360. February 24, 2016. https://www.waste360.com/waste-reduction/helping-austin-reach-zero-waste-through-inspiring-entrepreneurship.

Iwuoha, John-Paul. "Lorna Rutto–The innovative entrepreneur who creates wealth and jobs from plastic waste." Smallstarter. June 16, 2013. Accessed September 29, 2020. https://www.smallstarter.com/get-inspired/lorna-rutto/.

Lux, Heidi. "The U.S.'s largest trash hauler has stopped exporting plastic waste to other countries." Good.is. October 28, 2019. Accessed September 28, 2020. https://www.good.is/waste-management-plastic-trash-no-longer-shipped-abroad.

McCurry, Justin. "'No-waste' Japanese village is a peek into carbon-neutral future." *The Guardian*. March 20, 2020. https://www.theguardian.com/world/2020/mar/20/no-waste-japanese-village-is-a-peek-into-carbon-neutral-future.

Seven Generations International Foundation. "7th Generation Principle." Accessed September 28, 2020. http://7genfoundation.org/.

Singh, Jagdeep, Kyungeun Sung, Tim Cooper, Katherine West, and Oksana Mont. "Challenges and opportunities for scaling up upcycling businesses – The case of textile and wood upcycling businesses in the UK." *Resources, Conservation, and Recycling* 150, (2019). https://www.sciencedirect.com/science/article/pii/S0921344919303349#!

UN Environment Programme. "A future in recycling: from street waste collector to entrepreneur." March 11, 2020. Accessed September 28, 2020. https://www.unenvironment.org/news-and-stories/story/future-recycling-street-waste-collector-entrepreneur.

UpCycle Foundation. "About Us." Accessed September 28, 2020. https://upcyclefoundation.com/pages/about.

UpCycle Foundation. "UpCycle Foundation's Response to COVID-19." March 23, 2020. Accessed September 29, 2020. https://

upcyclefoundation.com/blogs/news/upcycle-foundations-re-
sponse-to-covid-19.

Yeh, Charlotte S., MD. "The power and prevalence of loneliness."
Harvard Health Blog. January 13, 2017. https://www.health.
harvard.edu/blog/the-power-and-prevalence-of-loneli-
ness-2017011310977.

AFTERWARD

American Forests. "Leading on Climate Change Solutions."
Accessed October 7, 2020. https://www.americanforests.org/
why-it-matters/climate/.

Carpenter, Michael. "Books vs ebooks: Protect the environment
with this simple decision." The Eco Guide. June 17, 2016. https://
theecoguide.org/books-vs-ebooks-protect-environment-sim-
ple-decision.

Do Something. "11 Facts about E-Waste." Accessed October 11,
2020. https://www.dosomething.org/us/facts/11-facts-about-
e-waste.

CPSIA information can be obtained
at www.ICGtesting.com
Printed in the USA
BVHW072312231220
596015BV00003B/8